Lucid Dreaming

Exercises To Explore Your Inner World, Overcome Fears & Unlock Your Creativity

(30 Minute Techniques For Dream Control, Memory, And Awareness)

Jamie Johnston

Published By **Tyson Maxwell**

Jamie Johnston

All Rights Reserved

Lucid Dreaming: Exercises To Explore Your Inner World, Overcome Fears & Unlock Your Creativity (30 Minute Techniques For Dream Control, Memory, And Awareness)

ISBN 978-1-77485-955-1

No part of this guidebook shall be reproduced in any form without permission in writing from the publisher except in the case of brief quotations embodied in critical articles or reviews.

Legal & Disclaimer

The information contained in this ebook is not designed to replace or take the place of any form of medicine or professional medical advice. The information in this ebook has been provided for educational & entertainment purposes only.

The information contained in this book has been compiled from sources deemed reliable, and it is accurate to the best of the Author's knowledge; however, the Author cannot guarantee its accuracy and validity and cannot be held liable for any errors or omissions. Changes are periodically made to this book. You must consult your doctor or get professional medical advice before using any of the suggested remedies, techniques, or information in this book.

Upon using the information contained in this book, you agree to hold harmless the Author from and against any damages, costs, and expenses, including any legal fees potentially resulting from the application of any of the information provided by this guide. This disclaimer applies to any damages or injury caused by the use and application, whether directly or indirectly, of any advice or information presented, whether for breach of contract, tort, negligence, personal injury, criminal intent, or under any other cause of action.

You agree to accept all risks of using the information presented inside this book. You need to consult a professional medical practitioner in order to ensure you are both able and healthy enough to participate in this program.

Table Of Contents

Chapter 1: what's lucid dreaming anyway? 1

chapter 2: the basics and practice of lucid dreaming 11

chapter 3: what is lucid dreaming, and how can it be used? 22

chapter 4: how to remember dreams 26

chapter 5: time distortion 33

chapter 6: inception 50

chapter 7: astral travel 67

chapter 8: taking control of the lucid dream 83

chapter 9: do's and don'ts to lucid dreaming 95

chapter 10: meditate your way to lucid dreams 101

chapter 11: the phases a sleep cycle 111

chapter 12: benefits and lucid dreaming 123

chapter 13: what is required for a dream life? 136

chapter 14: what your dreams are telling you, interpreting common symbols. Dreams with colors & numbers............ 151

chapter 15: scheduling for lucid dream 169

chapter 16: stepping into the dream world 179

Chapter 1: What's Lucid Dreaming Anyway?

If you aren't familiar with the term "lucid dreaming" or don't know exactly what it means, I'd love to give you a little explanation and show you why this phenomenon is so fascinating.

A lucid vision is a dream where you, as the dreamer, are aware that you are dreaming. This does not necessarily mean that you can control the dream at your will. However, it will eventually become possible.

Common mistakes I see are beginners thinking that lucid-dreaming is like an on/off switch. It's more of an array. There are normal dreams, which you have no control over, at one end. In the middle, maybe you wake up and realize that you are dreaming. But you don't have much control over your dreams so everything becomes blurred or hazy. At the other end, you're in total control. The dream is real and you can feel it with all your senses.

This book's goal is to guide you on the right spectrum of that spectrum. We want you to have as many long, lucid dreams and mind blowing experiences as possible.

Lucid dreams can differ from regular dreams in that you are aware of your surroundings. It is possible to consciously think, make decisions and influence the dream that you are in. This is quite different than a normal nightmare, which is more like a movie. While you can view and participate in what happens in your dream, you can't control the plot or outcome.

Here's the thing: Although you are conscious of your actions and can take control of them, you don't always have control over the actions and thoughts of others. Your subconscious mind is responsible for everything else. Imagine if you walked up to someone from your dream and began talking to them. Without you even being conscious of it, they'd start to talk back to you. Lucid dreaming can be far more fun than daydreaming. You'll always be amazed by what comes next.

If you've never had a lucid nightmare before, this might sound strange and frightening. Don't worry, lucid dreaming doesn't cause you harm. It won't disturb your sleep. Everybody can learn to luciddream. Even if you don't remember your dreams, everyone can. The science behind lucid dreaming has been proven real. It has been used for over 1000 years. Every year we learn more and more about the science of lucid-dreaming.

Lucid Dreaming: Why is it so Awesome?

I can't emphasize enough how incredible it is to be in a lucid dream.

Imagine being able live out all your wildest desires, and doing what you want, all the while it feels totally real.

Imagine being in a position to be able to travel to other worlds at night.

In my lucid dreams, everything I did was real, from being a professional soccer player to playing music with The Beatles. Nothing can compare to the experience of having a conversation between John Lennon and me in lucid dreams. Or at least that is what my brain interprets.

Here's my point. Each of us has things we desire to do but are simply not able. Not all of us will be famous musicians. We may not all be able visit the great Egyptian pyramids. All of us are not able to enjoy a romantic evening together with a supermodel. The possibilities are endless when you can lucid dream. If you can think of something, it is possible to make it happen. Only your imagination can limit you, and there are no limits to what you can do.

Someone making you mad? Send energy at them and turn them to dust.

You need to get places quickly. You can imagine a door behind you. It will be there when you turn your head. Inside the door is the place where you want to go.

Are you looking for someone to talk to? They are around the corner. Just walk around it and they'll be waiting for your return.

There are a million ways to make a lucid vision come true. I'll be discussing this in chapter four. However, I'm so excited for you all to experience the incredible power of luciddreaming.

I felt bored and unhappy for a long time. Wake up, go work, go to bed, and get up again. Repeat the same routine over and again. This is something that many of us feel. Once you learn to lucidly dream, however, this will cease to matter. Although our day-to-day routines aren't always the most exciting, it doesn't matter. But it doesn't really matter because we will get to live the life of our dreams every night.

Just for motivation, I want to share with you a few short excerpts from people's first dreams. These reports will allow you to get a taste of the emotion people feel when they have their first lucid vision. You won't believe it, but you will soon start lucid dreams regularly.

"Just wow. It was so amazing. It was like a dream. I can't wait until it happens again! I appreciate your time and tips.

"It's unexplainable, really.

I'm not believed by anyone so I want to share it here.

Lucid dreaming can be doubted by anyone. It was amazing even though it was difficult to control.

It gets easier to control, but we'll get to it later.

Here is the last story, which I wanted to share with all of you. It was told by someone who woke up from sleep.

"I laid there, with the biggest smile of my life. I turned to my girlfriend, and I said "I did that, I flew." She nodded in agreement and fell asleep. I was excited, however. In a dream, nothing has ever seemed so real. It is still amazing to me. "I could fly because I was in total control of my life!"

It will help you see the potential in lucid-dreaming and will provide you with lots of fun ideas once you've mastered the skill.

Warning: Patience IS Essential

You should be excited about what lies in store for you. It's quite difficult not to feel excited. It's hard not being overwhelmed by excitement when you discover that such an amazing power was hidden throughout your entire life.

You shouldn't be overly optimistic or expect too much, as that could lead to disappointment. Everything I have shared so far is accurate. Lucid dreams can be as fantastic as they're made out to, so there's no need for discussion.

Although it is possible for you to lucidly dream almost every night, it can be difficult. Lucid dreaming is something anyone could start one day. It's that amazing. You have to be able to lucidly dream whenever you wish. This can take some time, especially if it's difficult to recall your dreams right now.

Each person's experience with lucid dreaming will be different. Some people might have their first dream of lucidity tonight. For others, it may take more than six months to get your first lucid vision. I want you to know that it is not a good idea to compare yourself to others and get discouraged when you don't see immediate results. If you are willing to apply the knowledge in this book and truly want to succeed, it will happen.

I remember it took me around three months to experience my first lucid nightmare. It only lasted a few seconds. Keep in mind that although I didn't own a book like this one, it was a guide for me. After months of trying, I nearly gave-up. I am so glad I didn't, because without it I wouldn't have some of my most treasured memories, and I certainly wouldn't still be here writing this.

If you find yourself feeling discouraged or considering quitting, I recommend you go back to the book and read it again. You can also look up other people's experiences with lucid visioning. Let them demonstrate to you that it's worth the effort. You will be so grateful that you kept trying until it happens.

This will not be an easy task, but it will be life-changing. I promise you.

Chapter 2: The Basics And Practice Of Lucid Dreaming

What's it all about?

It is clear that you are dreaming. You control the outcome of events. It doesn't matter what. It's not as if lucid dreams are reality. So what's all the fuss about being aware that you are dreaming?

The very fact that you can fall asleep in a dream is a cool thing. Now you don't have to wake up feeling like 8 hours have gone by. Being conscious in an unconscious state can be both extraordinary and strange.

Lucid Dreaming is not just about novelty.

This is an ideal way to discover different fantasies that might not be possible in the real-world. Dreams often allow you to experience sexual fantasies and the ability to fly. Because this is a time and place where you can explore whatever you wish, without the need to be retorted in the real, waking universe.

Additionally, lucid dreams can be very useful in overcoming nightmares. Millions of people are plagued by terrifying, haunting nightmares. Sometimes they seem overwhelming and unavoidable. Giving the dreamer some control over the dreams can provide great relief.

However, lucid dreams will not automatically erase all nightmares. But they will become easier to manage. It's not as scary as it seems if you can actually see, understand, or engage with them directly.

Studies show that lucid dreams are seven-fold more likely to improve your dreams than make them worse. If this is not reason to give Lucid Dreaming a go, then I don't know what else.

You will learn how visualization can help you improve your lucid dreamsing skills later in this book. Lucid dreaming is also useful because it allows you to use your visualizations to improve your daily life. You can think of it as a dress rehearsal or a practice run. When you can imagine, feel, and experience how it feels to live that way, it is easier to see how you can achieve the same success in real life. This could be small things like improving your mood, or large changes like getting that high-paying career you have always wanted.

How do you know if you are dreaming lucidly?

As we have seen in the previous chapter, you can lucidly dream when you become aware of your dreaming and are able to control it. Although it sounds great on paper, what does it feel like in reality?

What's more, how can you make sure that you're doing it right?

If you've ever experienced any kind of dream in your lifetime (which is what everyone has), you'll know the vaguely fuzzy and ethereal feel that dreams give off. You cannot always be certain if what is being seen is full color or grayscale. People and places seem inexplicably to change in an instant.

Lucid dreams can look almost exactly the same. The trick is to awaken the part of your mind that can notice these subtle details. Notice the blurred scene instead of being crystal clear. Not only are the characters unusually grouped together, but the stairs leading to your front door seem to become an interminable flight of stairs that runs down the side a cliff.

The realization of these details will come suddenly if you can catch them while in the dream. It is possible that you might hear yourself say, "I am in the middle of my dream" or something similar.

This is where you want to be. This is when you will realize you are right in the middle or a lucid nightmare and you have complete control over everything.

Once you have reached the point where you are aware that your dream is real, you can start to create lucid dreams. Although it is simple to state, how can you actually lucidly dream?

Lucid dreams feel just like when you're awake, except it's happening while you're sleeping. For this reason, lucid dreaming can be used to change things in your dreams. Just think it!

What you imagine will come true. If you're looking to change your place, think "I want to go to the coast". If you are looking to bring someone else into your life, think "I wish my brother was there." It'll happen. You might find yourself in a paradise on the beach, or you may suddenly see your brother standing right beside you.

These are just a few ways to control your dream. However, the basic principle remains. Your mind is able to control the events just as well as your actions when awake.

The examples of visiting the beach and seeing your brother are only two options. You can choose anything you wish. We'll get back to it later. But remember, your imagination is your only limit.

Lucid dreaming

Now that you're familiar with what to look for when identifying a Lucid Dream, you can begin to create one.

Lucid dreams can happen by themselves - you might fall asleep in a natural way, but wake up to dream about it halfway through the night.

It'll be very unnerving the first time it happens. If you've never had one before, then the experience of being able and able to think while falling asleep is completely unnatural. However, spontaneous lucid dreams are rare and hard to come by so you might have to wait for your next one.

Inducing a ludicrous fantasy is something you can do by yourself. The more you practice, the more effective you will become. With a little luck you'll soon be able induce lucid dreams every evening - or as often as you want!

Your chances of success are increased if you create the ideal conditions for lucid dreams. Being lucid means you need to be deep asleep, so make sure you are as relaxed and comfortable as possible. Eliminate anything that might make you feel uneasy or interfere with your lucid dream experience.

Don't think that lucid sleep will be possible only if you have a lot of solid sleep. It is actually the opposite. The chances of having a lucid dream are greatly increased if you have a disturbed sleep.

You can think about this: While you're asleep, the boundaries between reality (reality) and dreams blur. These dreams are vivid enough to seem real and almost lifelike. You may find it helpful to place your consciousness at the threshold of sleep and waking in order to change your perceptions about reality.

The easiest way to accomplish this is to include both naps, and purposeful awakenings in your sleeping routine.

When it comes down to lucid dreaming, after-hours naps can be extremely successful. This is because lucid dreaming can be more successful when you have a short break.

These aspects of everyday life ensure that you won't go to sleep as quickly. These aspects of daily life mean that you won't fall asleep as deeply.

Problem with trying to lucid-dream during afternoon naps, is that they are often quite short. Even though there is no time limit for lucid dreams, it is more fun to be able stay longer to explore them. You may not have enough time for the lucid-dream experience to enjoy and appreciate if you take a quick power naps during your lunch break.

Better is to optimize your nighttime sleep. The easiest way to do this is to wake up every night.

It's a good idea to set your alarm an extra hour before you wake up. You must not leave your alarm on. Do not ignore it.

Keep your eyes open for half an hour to one hour after your alarm sounds. There is no need to get up to do high-energy tasks. You can stay calm and relax while you practice self-awareness techniques. We'll discuss these later. But for now, keep calm and relaxed while focusing on the task at hand.

Let yourself go to sleep for half an hour to one hour. If you are awake for only a few minutes, your mind will be ready to go into lucid dream mode. If you can inject this short time of sleep into your night, the chances of experiencing an lucid dreams increase by between 15 and 20 times.

If you are still not sure about how awake or sleepy you need to get, don't worry. You don't want to wake up exhausted and then fall into deep sleep.

Instead, try to get a sleep that is broken. This will allow you to wake up from a sleepless night, but not enough to feel fully awake.

Chapter 3: What Is Lucid Dreaming, And How Can It Be Used?

When man dreams, he is genius.

I walked through the parking lot, passing a bike with a massive speaker embedded in its seat. This should have been a trigger. The clerk was there when I arrived at the counter and immediately saw me. He looked at me and asked for my name. I saw him enter it into his ledger. The name in his ledger that was above mine was the exact same as mine. He began to scream at the book and to pound his head into it. I suddenly realized that I was dreaming. The building disappeared. Rob

**

Lucid Dreaming can be described as the state when you're asleep, dreaming, but are conscious of your own self. Lucid Dreaming simply means being aware of the fact that you're dreaming while dreaming. It gives people the chance to do things that are otherwise impossible. Lucid dreams are a gift that allows you to see your true self and maximize your potential.

The term "lucid" refers to having a clear head. It also means that you are in an understanding state when it comes to dreaming. This is important because it will help you achieve your ultimate goal, which is to be able control your dreams and enjoy all that comes with them.

You can't control your dreams overnight. But it is something you can learn if you commit to the suggestions in this book. It is possible to change, add, modify, or shift your dream in any way you wish. This can be quite an experience. You can make your imagination a stronger tool in every aspect of your life by creating a dreamworld. As an Olympic athlete trains their skills and builds muscles, your imagination could also be developed and used as a strength in your daily life.

Before I proceed, I want to dispel a common myth. Lucid Dreaming isn't a new age concept. It has been mentioned and written about for over 100 years by the scientific and psychology community.

The Marquis d'Hervey wrote one of the earliest published works on lucid-dreaming. He published his book Dreams: How to Guide them in the late nineteenth-century. This first work was the result of years of personal research. It also included records of his dreams. In his book, d'Hervey discussed the evolution of his ability and ability to control events and circumstances in dreams. Following the same steps, he first practiced recalling his dream and then became aware of his dreams. Finally, he controlled the situations. His work demonstrated that anyone can achieve lucid visioning with just a little effort.

Many psychological and scientific studies confirm that there is a link between the dream and real worlds. They date back at most to Dreams and How to Guide Them.

The relationship may not be one of physicality (although some would disagree), but it is definitely one of mentality. Numerous studies have linked real-life problem resolution to dream/nightmare confrontations or resolution.

Chapter 4: How To Remember Dreams

Three stages are required to be able remember your dreams. The first stage involves what you do before getting to sleep.

Stage One – Before Bed

At this stage, it is important to have a consistent bedtime and wake-up time. This will ensure you get a good night sleep and that you are relaxed while sleeping. While you're sleeping, it's important that there aren't any outside noises, pets, or people around.

Step 1: Length of time

Make sure to have at least eight hours sleep each night. This will ensure you have enough time for REM sleep multiple times in one evening.

Step Two - Environment

A peaceful and comfortable environment is essential for sleep. Avoid noises and distractions that could keep you awake, or make it difficult to fall asleep. Wearing earplugs can help you to fall asleep faster.

Step Three: Recording Device

It doesn't matter if you have a pencil and some paper or an actual audio recorder. You want something that you can reach when you get up in the morning. Remember that dreams are most vividly remembered when we wake up.

Step Four – Alarm

Keep your alarm close by your bed to ensure you can remember your dreams. The more you move, the more likely you are to forget about your dreams. This is because your brain is switching brainwaves from one stage or another.

Step Five: Avoid stimulants

Do not eat, drink, or take any medication that may keep you awake. You should avoid eating, drinking, and taking medications a few hours before your bedtime so you don't disrupt your sleep.

Step Six: Meditate

But you don't have necessarily to sit in lotus posture and meditate. Instead, take some deep, calming breaths before getting into bed. This puts you in a good place and helps you forget any worries from the day. Take your laptop, tablet, or phone with you to bed.

Step Seven – Make a Conscious decision

It is more likely that you will remember your dreams if it is something you say to yourself. Before you go to bed, say out loud or mentally to yourself that you will remember and cherish your dreams.

Step 8 - Think About Your Problems

After you feel relaxed and are able to remember your dreams clearly, take a moment to reflect on any difficulties or decisions you may have. Try not to think of solutions. You may be surprised to find a solution in your dreams.

The Morning After is Stage 2.

There are a few things that you can do to make your dreams come true.

Step One - Concentrate

After waking up, try to keep the same position and your focus on the object in front of you. You should go through your entire dream. Keep track of every detail and gaze at the object. The object will become visible to you later, and you'll be able recall the majority of your dream.

Step Two - Keep it in writing

You can either set a pencil and notebook next to your bed or an audio recording device. Once you have grabbed the item, start to capture every detail of the dreams. The location, plot, people and emotions involved will all need to be recorded. Note any images you are able to recall.

You should also write down dialog from your dream. This might be the best thing to do because words are what you will remember most about your dream. Do not write down anything you don't remember from the dream. This could trigger a recollection later.

Stage Three – Throughout Day

It is possible to recall and trigger information about your dream at any time during the day.

Step 1: Record them

Keep your recorder and notepad with you all day to capture any dreams you might recall. Sometimes, something as small as the smell of coffee and a sound can trigger memories of our dreams.

Step two - Go back to bed

Sometimes you can recall the dream vividly if the object is placed in the same spot you were in during the dream. If you have latent memories, it is a good idea to open your eyes and see what the object was.

Step 3 - Put it into practice

This will take practice. It might not work the first time. Make sure you go to bed and rise at the same times every day. You also need to have a recording device with you at all times. You might also like to study your dreams in order find patterns and decipher the meanings. Take note of the food you ate the night before to determine if this has affected your dreams.

Chapter 5: Time Distortion

A watched pot never boils, have you ever heard that expression? If you haven't, fill a pot full of cold water and place it on the stove. Next time you have an opportunity, set a stopwatch and wait for it boil. Make sure to not talk to others, look at your stopwatch, read on your phone or do anything else that could distract you.

It depends on the temperature and humidity of the water as well as atmospheric pressure, humidity and initial volume. The rate at which thermal energy gets transferred into the water can also affect the time it takes. A small pot of cold water will likely boil in 10 minutes.

The experiment is now complete. Then, pour the boiling water into the pot. Wait for it to boil. You can't do anything while it boils.

It seems like a very long time. Yet, the stopwatch shows that it took only a few moments.

Truth is, our perceptions of time are not constant. There are activities you can do that seem to drag out time, while others make it seem like it passes in a blink of an eye.

The worst part? Unless you have the skills to manage it, the boring, monotonous activities that we don't like to do take the longest. It's the fun, exciting activities that are easy to control and disappear quickly.

This is good news when dreaming.

Our minds can adjust how much time is perceived. That's why we experience those effects when waiting for something or when having fun. It's simply that most people don't know what to do.

This is because our unconscious mind drives it. Our unconscious mind drives our dreams.

This leads to the conclusion that, if you want to spend a lot time in your dreams, often all you have to do to make sure we are there when we plan.

As an example, let's say we start our plans with this statement:

Tonight I dreamed that I would spend an entire day on a 45 foot sailboat sailing around Bermuda.

Then, you add the details about how long we plan to spend on each activity. As soon as we do this, our unconscious minds will automatically tell us how much time it takes to accomplish each task.

We have many other ways in hypnosis that we can increase the time that you perceive. I won't get into details here, as it is usually enough to place the intention in your dreams.

The Self-Hypnosis Process, which I discuss in my book The Self-Hypnosis Form, can cause significant amounts time distortion.

Your dream lab

Imagine you have a dream to learn something. Perhaps you're looking for creative solutions for a problem. Maybe you're looking for a way to exercise your physical abilities.

How do you do it? By creating what I call a dream laboratory within your plan.

It's a lab that I have labeled, but this is mostly because it is my laboratory. Your lab can be labelled as whatever suits you.

If you're passionate about a sport it's likely to be more beneficial for you to find a suitable place to practice that sport.

It doesn't matter if you want to learn a craft.

The important thing is to design your laboratory to fit the task in hand.

Because I am both a scientist and hypnotist, the setting for my dream lab is an ancient castle made of stone. There are lab benches and bubbling concoctions using tubing, conical flasks, and tesla coils. It is equipped with all manner of technological gadgets and the ability to summon scientists from any era. And the future.

It's easy to build your dream lab. All you need is to decide what it will be used for. Then, create a plan.

First, you need to decide what your dream laboratory is for. This could be for any purpose. It could be, for example, a driving course, where you can practice your golf swings. You can also choose to play a full course of golf with many different holes. You are free to pick. It's not a fixed decision. You can alter it at any point you choose.

If you are an artist, feel free draw on a piece paper what your idea will look like.

Now, make a plan.

Tonight's dream will take me to my woodworking workshop. It has a large area with a drill press and a lathe. Every tool is visible hanging on the walls. I am able to see all my tools grouped in an organized manner so I only have to look up to find what I need. Today I practice using the lathe to turn a difficult piece jarrah. I am paying attention to how the wood reacts when I cut it. It takes me 12 hours to get the right setting on my lathe. This room will be my woodworking shop whenever I return to it in the future.

I am sure you get the concept. In this case, you'd need to be familiar with using a lathe to turn jarrah. If you don't, your brain won't have anything to latch on to and will make up random crap. This can be entertaining, but not helpful when trying to learn a skill.

The last sentence is used to establish a label for the dream lab. Names are used to identify our dream environments. This creates a framework in our minds that makes it easier to return to the same place in future. This is what we wish to see in a dream lab.

When we are ready to make a return to our woodworking workshop in the future, we only need to mention it at the beginning our dream plan.

I can't help but dream that I'm in my woodworking shop tonight when I wake up.

Don't waste your time with useless stuff

I'm going making a prediction. You'll soon find other lucid dreamers making claims that might seem inconsistent with what you've actually experienced.

The key to all this is to ask yourself whether it actually makes sense.

Here are some recent examples.

First, as I said, I've heard it claimed that you cannot read books from your dreams. This could even be used as a way to verify that you are dreaming.

If you have a copy in your mind, there is no reason to not be able read it in a dream. The only thing you can't do is to read a book which you haven't yet read.

If the information is in your head, then all you need is to ask. If you've ever had that information in some form or another, it's going to be there.

Take, for example, a book. The contents of the book will largely reside in your unconscious mind if you have ever read it.

Also, if the book is not in your hands, you cannot dream up a clone. This may be why I believe you cannot read a book while dreaming.

This is important because as you go on more lucid dreaming, you'll almost certainly learn from others. If someone says you can tell when you are dreaming by the fact that your dream books are always instabile or lack words, then you might conclude that you may be awake while actually dreaming.

Similar to the previous claim, you can also tell if your dream is real by simply flicking a light button and noting that it stops working. I can tell you that light switches, and other technological devices, always work in dreams. These devices don't always function in the waking realm. This is a sign they are not doing a good job.

It is easy to test whether what you are doing is something that has been experienced while awake.

If it is, then you know what to do and can choose to follow that path in your dreams.

Let's now get to the point: Reality checks.

Reality checks

We can dream and it can seem real. If we want to manipulate our dreams, we will need a method to find out if we are dreaming.

This is accomplished with a reality assessment.

A reality check is, at its core, nothing but a test we can take in our waking life and in our dreams. It allows us to evaluate whether or not we can act differently in our dreams.

Reality checks can be challenging because you have to remember how to do it in your dreams so you can see what you are really dreaming.

Recalling earlier in this book will help you to recall that dreams tend to contain things we experience before we sleep, as well as those that we experience throughout our day.

Conveniently we can use it to make sure that reality checks are performed in our dreams.

This is the first step to making it happen. There is so much to choose from, I suggest that you start with something simple. For example, you can push a finger into your palm and expect it to move all the way. You can do whatever you want, but it shouldn't cause any injuries to anyone.

It is important to choose something that is not possible in your real world.

Once you have selected something to do you will want to continue doing it throughout your day. There are many ways to accomplish this.

If you have a structured day, it may be possible to conduct your reality check at the beginning or end of certain activities. It could be a ritual that you use to begin every meeting, for example, if your day is full of meetings. The problem with this is that it will be difficult to see the reality of your dreams in the event you have a vision of a meeting.

A reminder alarm can be useful if your schedule is not as structured. Make sure to not set an alarm that goes off while you're sleeping.

All you need to do now is to perform your reality-check and watch what happens.

When we do this enough we find that reality checks are automatic.

Remember how we talked earlier about memory and how it works? It all comes down to association. Reality checks work on two levels. It is important to practice them daily so that we can easily recall them when we dream about them. The second is to have them associated with as many other things as we might dream of so that when we do dream about those things, it automatically checks that they are real.

When we perform our reality checks as an automatic process in the waking realm, it is very likely that we will continue to do so in our dreams.

Next, perform your reality test in your dream. It will work. This is your sign to enter your dream world, become lucid, or use your dream any way that suits you.

To make it concrete, I'll show you an example. Last night, after writing out my usual dream plan, I was struck by the thought of this book I'm currently reading. I fell asleep and woke the next day.

I did not think about it too much and got up to write on my computer.

Since I've written a book about it, you might assume that I have been lucidly dreaming for years. As a result, I have many reality checks habits. One is that while I am using my computer, I place my hand on the desk and check to see if it passes.

So I wrote a few sentences. Then, my hand automatically pressed on the desk. I quickly read through the document. I knew then that I was in a dream and I woke from my dream.

Look at your own life and you'll find many examples of things you can use as reality checkers. When you build enough habits around them, they will begin to happen naturally in your day and in your dreams.

Safety and hallucinations

Reality checks can be misleading. It is possible to choose what we wish to see in our dreams. If we hallucinate, however, this may also apply to the waking world.

For example, I discussed earlier the reality check of pushing your finger through the palm. This won't work for us in our waking world. We can, however, hallucinate to believe that it did work.

This possibility means that we cannot be 100% certain that our brains are awake.

This has a very important consequence. It is vital to not do anything while we are asleep that could cause significant harm to others or ourselves.

Let me use an example to illustrate. Let's suppose you've made the decision to fly. You realize you are living in a fantasy.

You are, in fact, wide awake and hallucinating.

Then you will expect to fly if you climb to the top.

SPLAT.

It's not right.

It doesn't mean that you can't dream. Just be careful. Do not jump from high buildings, but instead take off from below.

Do not run away and kill people, or smash into walls with your car at speed. If you do not want someone in your life, tell them to go.

It's your dreams and you can choose what happens.

Even if you weren't awake and hallucinating, your dreams can cause you to damage things in your life.

Chapter 6: Inception

Your dream world can be yours. What if I said that there's a way for you to enter someone else's dream universe? This chapter is called inception.

You might have seen Leonardo Dicaprio's Inception. What do YOU think about this? Is it possible for someone to live their dream? Is it possible to give people a specific dream?

How is this possible?

Inception depicts how they used chemicals to get into people's heads. It's sci-fi. That is not how the real inception works.

It is possible to send a thought to someone and have them experience it as if it were a dream. It is only the vibration of thought which makes it possible. We are in an ocean of frequency, energy, and vibration.

You and I are in the ocean of it. Each of us is only a whirlpool. It is no secret that our thoughts broadcast every time. However, only people who are within the same frequency range can "catch" the broadcast.

You will answer "What is my mind?" You will make predictions. It is possible to solve it by reading non-verbal signals and micro-expressions. This could lead to you failing. If you do this, your conscious mind interprets my expressions. This disables your "invisible antenna". It is best to relax and let the information flow.

To disable your receiving ability, the button is to think that "I know" (or "What's it?"). I have repeatedly conducted this experiment with different people. I found that anyone can send information to another person just by imagining (not through thinking) that he delivers the information package. The target then imagines that the information package is delivered to him. This is my view of the core principle of telepathy.

Two people sat side by side at about 6 feet distance. I gave them specific roles. The sender was A and the recipient was B. I caused light trance in both of them. Before that, the A had drawn on the paper something that he believed he only knew. In the light state of trance, they were instructed by the B to imagine that they complete the transaction (the paper). After that, B drew his image and then B's picture confirmed the A.

Telepathy is the ability to send and receive thoughts using imagination. Telepathy can only work if both parties are aware of their roles. They should both know what each other do. You can't send thoughts to someone without knowing that you do.

Each person also has a protective field that protects them from external thoughts vibrations. What is the best way to inception?

You won't believe I sent an orgasmic vision to a girl as a child. It was true. I was taught how to chant a mantra with peppercorns between the thumb and index of my thumb. It was total witchcraft, so I won't go into it. It was just truth. It was possible. Another method to send magical dreams is to chant a mantra, imagine the person, then light-blowing the pillow. It worked flawlessly. This is another form of witchcraft. The essence of witchcraft is the exact same. It was because we were in the same ocean. Our interconnectedness is what makes us all so special.

Can we send someone a dream without being a witch or a wizard? Two techniques will be taught to you in this chapter. Wait. What I mean here is the lucid vision.

Stealth Call to the Operator

Do you recall the operator we spoke of in the last chapter? That's all. It's that simple. This is achieved by using conversational Hypnosis. This course will show you how to infuse someone's subconscious with a lucid dreams command.

You are aware that trance is necessary to allow you to interact with an operator. The process works in a similar way to the COP except for a few minor differences. You don't have the goal in a trance. It is enough to "read" signs that the target is in the trance.

SCOP is something children often experience. Telling them a horror story will cause nightmares. Their conscious mind is less critical than that of an adult. This can also be observed in the SCOP. This makes the target less important.

Preparing your Dream Images

You should think about three things. The dream's figure, the scene, and what the dream is about. To give the target a romantic kiss on their lips on the beach, for example.

However, you won't reveal it to your target. You will place it in stealth. The normal way is to say "I want you have a dream that you kiss me on the lips when you are on a beach". But in stealth mode, you each send the command to the operator individually. Just prepare your dream images. Keep it brief!

Surpassing the Critical Area

The critical area, or the edge between the conscious and subconscious minds, is called the critical area. This is why the target must be in complete trance to avoid it. This is known as alert-trance.

You must choose the right time, and the right place. The perfect time to relax is after lunch, dinner or on vacation. The ideal place is one where you will not be distracted.

Invite the target's target to discuss what interests them or items that bring back strong emotions. Talk about her favorite songs and colors. People tend to be more open and less critical of others, and their mental-defense tends lower when they talk about the things they love. They feel more secure and open to sharing their thoughts. They feel safer because they can talk about or think about their true knowledge.

Interrupt her speech to ask questions and guide the target into an instant trance. This must be done during her sentence. Do this before she reaches the end of her sentence. You should not do this often, as it could give the impression that she is not appreciated. Be wise.

As you can see, when she is suddenly stopped her eyes will go completely blank for a short time. This is the trance gateway. This is Bandler's handshake interrupt technique that I modified for speaking interruption.

It is common for people to forget where they are supposed to go when they speak and then suddenly stop. This happens due to the trance. The trance will make you forget, but then you'll lose your words. This is the moment when your subconscious mind is open and you are able to pay attention (automatically). Do you agree with me?

Phone the Operator

Now, let me tell you the operator's name. Your mother's name when you were young (1-7 years) is the operator's name. If you are interrupted, be sure to call the target's operator. It is okay to ask the target if you don't know. It's not privacy. It could be Emma, the name of your target's operator. This can be done during the first interruption.

"Wait... How were you called when your childhood began? Emma? So, Emma... I call Emma now. Go on ..."

Because you are calling the operator, you won't be saying "I call Emma", but "I call Emma". Once you have done this, the operator begins listening to your voice. Next, you will need to execute your next interruption.

Sending Codified Images of the Dream

It is essential that the dream images be represented or codified and in the correct position. It is possible to send each image one by one, but if you don't have time for a long conversation, then send two images at once. Here is the structure.

Sleeping time - Emma, at which time do you normally sleep?

Your face : Emma. Can you imagine your face if I close your eyes?

Kiss her: [Look at the lips of her while you kiss your lips] [no words and very brief]

The beach + dreams - Emma, what is the most beautiful sandy beach that you have ever seen?

You can ask her questions to continue her story. You can also ask about any other subjects that interest you. Once you are done, you can "lock", the command by calling the usual name of the woman and not the operator.

You have just learned the SCOP technique, which is the first inception technique. This technique only works if you are skilled at communicating. This technique can be used to help you improvise. Don't be boring, be funny, be open-minded, be respectful, and be appreciative.

The Dream Intrusion

Before I share this powerful technique with you, I want you to know that I cannot be held responsible for any damages that you may cause. You are about learn how to enter another person's dream universe. You might end up hurting yourself. I warned.

Telepathy is the fundamental principle that underpins this technique. After many successful experiments with students, I designed it to allow me to send a remote dream. I realized that lucid dreams can be used to induce dreams in the target's mind by entering their dream world through lucid dreaming.

This technique works in your lucid visioning. It means that you enter another's dream in your lucid dreaming.

You can use any technique (MILD, CA, WILD, COP, or WILD) that you find most effective. I will not repeat the lucid-dream procedures to anyone else.

However, you must clearly state your intent. Your goal is to unlock the door to your target's dream universe. Oh my God, I don't believe you will ever see it.

Requirements

For this technique to work correctly, you must have three things. They are:

Knowing the sleep cycles, time and length of the target;

Creating a basic dream scenario or dream plan.

The lucid dreaming is a state of being in complete control.

If the target is asleep in her final sleep cycle, it's possible to enter her dream. If the timing is off, the door will not open.

So that you can know what to do once you've reached your destination, the basic dream plan is very important. While you can modify it once it is there, it isn't always easy. It is not your world anymore.

It's not possible to achieve this feat with only your imagination. You have to be in the same mental state (dreaming and sleep) as your target. It is all about frequency synchronization.

A sample case

This is how my experience with The Dream Intrusion Technique worked for me. I was invited into the dreams of one my students. When I attempted to unlock the door, it locked. After a while the door opened.

I saw him lying on his back, but the scene is very different. I saw a different scene and I woke up. I told him "I am entering your dream. Tomorrow, I would like you to tell me more about this dream.

I left that message and he went back to bed. I closed the door, and I quit. I didn't tell anything to him the next morning. I waited to hear his story, but he didn't tell me. He appeared at night, and told me: "Last night was the night I dreamed that you were there. You came and you sang one song. I don't remember which song. Then, I woken up."

Look. You may find your dreams mixed up with other things. You may have a different dream than your target. It could be the result of the target having had different thoughts or intentions before he fell asleep. Repeating the message or performing the action may help to ensure that your messages are received clearly.

Warnings

I warned you, you can intrude on the dreams of someone else's life. Here are the risks you need to be aware of.

First of all, it's dangerous for your safety if your target wakes up suddenly while you're still in your dream. You will experience total darkness and confusion. You will feel very sleep paralysed. The next day, you will have a terrible headache.

It is risky if your target is dreaming before you get in the doorway. It's fine if the dream is positive. It's not good if your target is in a terrible situation. If that happens, it will be your nightmare for a very long period.

Thirdly because you are going through two levels, it is important to exit your dreaming state intentionally. Otherwise, you may experience psychosis. Even if you're awake, your mind may still be dreaming. This is what makes you confused.

Fourth, if the goal of your actions is not clear (to locate the target's dreamworld doorway), you might be tempted to enter a unknown field that could cause mental harm.

Last, even though your message and intention are positive, the messages may look different in the dream of your target. Let's take, for instance, the scenario where you give a flower but your target dreams that you touch her. This will affect your credibility.

Before you take on this risk, you need to be aware of the consequences. It is impossible to control the outcomes of your dreams in this world. You cannot control the outcome of your dreams when you enter another person's. If you find yourself in someone else's world, their rules will prevail, not yours.

Chapter 7: Astral Travel

Although astral travel is just another term for astral projecting, many people mistake it as something entirely different. It's exactly the same thing.

If I had said that I have an attral body a few centuries back, I might have been burned at my stake twice. I would have also been burned if I disclosed that I could fly on and see the future or hear people's thoughts. People looked at my astral senses as though I was a 'gaga'. I even got stared at by them as recently as twenty-years ago, when I openedly spoke about them. As a kid, I can recall playing a game with myself and later with a group. I would sit in a corner, near the ceiling, and observe other people's interactions. I found it a fun activity that I enjoyed and could do all by myself. I did this with no thought, completely unaware of the fact that my astral self was floating above me. It was part of me. I used to believe that someone else should do what my abilities before I realized how different it was. I did not tell anyone about this. To be able to talk about my inner life and other aspects, I had the responsibility to ensure that I was around the right people in a safe environment. Today, "astral travel" has become a buzzword all over the internet. Numerous people are now interested in astral projection. It is possible that both true and false, every second person I meet claims to be able to "astral fly" or have had an out of body experience. Some people fly while they are meditating, resting, or while lucidly dreaming. As a result, many people have experienced near-death experiences.

Traditional research is not yet able to keep up with hidden, esoteric wisdom that dates back thousands upon thousands of years. Many scientists are also excluded from this esoteric realm of science. But it is opening up due to the sheer number of people who believe in and act. However, human knowledge is the key to understanding and feeling things. Scientists, physicists, and others are following the mystical movement in greater numbers than ever. The metaphysical physicists who are emerging are increasing in number and have greater weight as they are physicists. This is great news, and it happens at a reasonable time.

A mystic is someone who believes there are other planes of reality, but is not interested in learning about them. This is the case for most saints. An occultist, on the other hand, is someone who believes and does extensive studies and experiments. Edgar Cayce. Pythagoras. C. W. Leadbeater. And Gopi Krishna are just a few of the well-known occultists. There are hundreds of other well known occultists both in the eastern or western realms. There are also thousands more scattered across the globe. These beings may be aware of or in contact with other realms.

Here's what I found while searching the internet for astral travel.

It's hard to refuse such a wonderful invitation.

Unfortunately, many people still believe they can visit other worlds. I hope you find this informative and interesting. You can read more about astral travel and continue your writing.

According to the most recent and oldest mystic teachings there are seven different planes of existence. The material plane is lowest, while the planes of forces are second and so forth. The astral and mental planes are both known. We won't discuss the three other planes, as we are focusing on the astral. But it would be useful if you could confirm that each plane has seven subplanes. And each subplane has seven subdivisions. It's up to you to do the calculations.

These planes can't be made of matter. They're also not made up of a succession of straight layers. The planes can be ranked by their respective levels of energy vibration. Matter has a lower level of energy vibration. These planes are interconnected in the one point of space. An ancient teacher once said that "a plane is not a place but a condition of being". Physics students are well aware that every point in space contains vibrations of heat and light of various colors, as well as electricity. Each frequency of vibration is unique and doesn't interfere with others. A ray or sunray is a rainbow composed of different colors. Each one vibrates at their own pace and does not dominate the other. Prana or the 'vital' force can be contained in the plane.

In occult teachings, it is often mentioned that the astral areas and their occupants and phenomena are important. Astral regions are vibrational representations in the astral plane that share space and do not interfere. The Greek word for "astral" is "related to a Star". It was used initially to describe the Greek heavens which are the Gods' home. Due to this expanded meaning, the word 'ghostland' came to refer to 'ghostland. They believed this ghost-land was populated with angelic creatures of higher order and disembodied souls. The terminology used by oriental occultists was borrowed from ancient Sanskrit. Although these terms were more complicated than the Greek terms, they preferred to use them because they were easier to understand for western students.

They began to understand the astral and other aspects that existed in ancient times. This understanding was lost as humanity advanced and became increasingly materialistic, culminating with the twentieth century.

There are two ways you can reach the astral world. You can use the astral senses or communicate with your astral body. Every man has an astral counterpart to his physical senses that works on the astral plane, just as the physical senses do on the material. With the help of the five astral senses, anyone can see, hear and smell on an astral plane. Some people have two additional senses, which are astral counterparts to the five. It is possible to teach almost anyone how to develop these astral perceptions.

Practice can help develop astral sight or the ability of seeing by astral sight. A blind woman is being tended to in a familiar setting. After her surgery, she was capable of identifying the operating room in detail, along with the names of the doctors and nurses. She could also identify their faces and the colors of their eyes. Even though she was anesthetized she could tell us which doctor operated on her and how many assisted. She could also repeat interactions she had with them while she was working. This was a mystery to doctors, but not to the occultist. Because of her astral sight and ears, she clearly saw and heard all things. She had lost her eyesight, but not her astral sight. She had separated her astral and real bodies, and was floating in an operating room, looking at all that was going.

However, most clairvoyants experience astral vision bursts. However, a qualified occultist is able to move between different sets of senses at will. The occultist can simultaneously work on both of these planes with enough practice. Clairvoyants don't have to be in a trance or leave their bodies to experience the astral plane. What she has to do to feel the astral world is to change her perspective.

Another option is traveling to the astral realm. The person leaves his body and enters his or her astral body in order to fly on the thetral plane. The astral bodies are made up of an extremely high frequency ethereal material. It is neither matter or power, but something in between. While it may outlive the human body by many decades, the astral bodies is a carbon replica of it. It is not immortal, and like the physical body, will eventually fall apart. Advanced occultists will be able to leave their physical bodies (which are usually in sleep or coma) and travel to any place in the astral realm at will. On the other side, the astral bodies are connected to their actual bodies by a thin, cobweblike rope of invisible matter. It expands and contracts according to his movement away from it or towards it. Accidents on the astral body can cause the filament to burst and his actual body will be permanently lost. However, accidents like these do occasionally happen. Obscurt tradition provides evidence of such incidents occurring only once in a while. There have been reports that astral bodies get stuck on the ether plane and are unable for extended periods of time to return to their earthly body. The human body has been declared dead and buried. I will leave it up to imagination to imagine the consequences if and when this astral body makes it back to its real body. Talk about a nightmare for the poor soul!

The astral plane is just as natural and set up as the real world. Steam is also as natural as water, ice and sand. The astral plane has a landscape that is as solid and solid as anything they can see. Like the physical worlds of earth, the astral realm has its own unique geography, shapes, objects, and other features. The rule of Change is applicable to both the astral world and the material world. As with the natural realms, the astral also has its own rules. If these rules are not followed, both the occupants and visitors of the astral realm will be affected. The astral world is just like the real one. There are continents as well as points in space, countries, places, realms and nations. Simply by wanting to fly from Zurich or Bombay, one could do this in a split second. If you have the skill and strength to fly, you can navigate all sub-planes one at a time, look at the people and their activities, return to the physical world in a matter of seconds, or even faster. You can also descend to and fly with the astral body to any physical location that you choose to visit friends or loved ones.

You will come across many strange people as you travel through the astral realm. Sometimes, astral shells, and even apparent spirit forms, can be mistaken for deceased loved ones. Astral shells are astral dead bodies. They can also be called "astral corpses". Artificial beings are made by those who have strong religious beliefs, like a mother praying to the angels for her son. Angel shapes take on physical form in these situations and can function on the astral plane. Many family ghosts were created and kept alive by simply telling the exact same story over and again, and believing that they exist. This is how haunted house stories are explained. These entities may be kept alive by believing and thinking repeatedly. If they don't, they will eventually die. Existences on planes in the astral realm aren't humans. These beings are not visible to the human eye, but astral sight can detect them in certain circumstances.

On the astral plane, there is no time, space or hindrance. You can do so much in a second, pass through walls, and fly between ends of the planet in a matter a minute. It is possible to travel through time and fly. You have probably experienced much of this at least once in your dream. You will meet guardian spirits as well as long-deceased family members. It is all fine. You have two options. One, you can astral travel unknowingly or ignore it. Two, you can remember it in a dream. It would be beneficial if you were able to astral travel in a state of mind. It is clear that you and I can do all of these things and more. People are often not ready for such situations and may become paranoid if they are forced to.

It is believed that very evolved souls astral-travel with their celestial mentors at midnight. Their bodies rest well so they can attend spiritual courses that offer advanced spiritual teachings. Indigo girls, who are advanced spirits that have reincarnated, often attend supernatural schools after their physical bodies fall asleep. While Indigo children are not new to history, many are present today in large numbers to aid mankind in the extraordinary change loop.

It is false to think that astral visions appear out of thin air. The rest of it is a steady and slow process. Many people are affected by it but don't have the right training to make it better. Many people experience astral perception from time to another. If you feel the need to test out the various techniques available online, this is what you should do. Don't listen to anyone asking you to join them when you travel through the astral world. You could be lured into staying. Instead, instead, look forward and not backward. Look upward, rather than down. Fear attracts negativity. Therefore, it is crucial that you have faith and don't be afraid. A sliver or the Divine Flame is within you, and it will protect you.

It is impossible to know if someone will teach you how fly on the astral flight plane in twenty minutes. This was reported on one of the websites. Some people with extremely advanced levels may be able do so. Everyday we witness miracles. But, what if you can be hypnotized and made to believe that you are traveling through an astral plane, and then told to recall everything you heard during the hypnosis. This will actually happen. All I can say is to be cautious and watchful. The less risky an activity is, the greater your ability to see things clearly. If you are easily pessimistic or fearful, I advise you to stay clear. Some gurus believe that untrained novices are at risk when they travel to the astral planes alone.

Chapter 8: Taking Control Of The Lucid Dream

Believe You Can

If you think you are dreaming, then you are at the edge a bluff and need to fly. Trust that you can do it, you might. Realize that you're in a dream and must fly. However, you will still fall. You might think that falling will be painful.

You can only trust what you're thinking in your dream world. If you have confidence in yourself, everything you do will happen. Lucid will also help you escape fear and allow you to build a stage that allows you to achieve the incomprehensible things you've always imagined.

Start A Fantasy Diary

A reliable idea about your fantasies and dream memory are two of the keys to turning out to being Lucid. Both of these are possible by keeping a fantasy diary. A fantasy journal can be as simple or complex as a spiral-bound notebook. Existing is just that. You should keep your journal and a pen close to where you go to sleep each night. You should keep a detailed record of your fantasies. It is important to include as many details as possible. Each morning, take the time to go through your diary pages and review each fantasy. As you begin to write down more of your evening tasks, you will find that you often dream about the exact same things. A succession of dreams may include your sister or pet, the sea and school, snakes, or anything else. These repeating components of your dreams are known as dream sign and they are a great way to start to have Lucid dreams. Your fantasies may contain certain individuals, events, areas, or circumstances that you don't know about. This is why dream after dream can appear over and over again. You can identify these individual dream signs and they will be available as tourist spots in the fantasy realm, which is an incredible way to get clarity.

Perform the Rude Awakenings during the Day

Material science can, in general get fluffy in dream, except for Lucid Dreaming. Rude awakenings are helpful in determining if we are dreaming. You can start this process by having brief rude awakenings in your consciousness. As you enter a space, switch the light switch off and on a few times. Do this slowly and carefully. Be aware of your surroundings and pay attention to what you're doing. Find two to three unexpected awakenings that you are used to. Then, you can easily accept them as part of your journey to Lucidity in your dreaming.

My most favorite rude awakenings are when I take a look at the ground and feel that gravity is holding me down. I recognize a Lucid dream when I have one. I'm ready to fly a few steps off the ground. If you want to become Lucid at evening, then perform ten severe awakenings every day.

The question, "Am i dreaming?" can be asked to yourself. You'll start asking similar questions while you are in a dream.

Things being what are, you can often tell if someone is dreaming. This is because the trick involves halting and thinking about the situation. While it may sound absurd to question this when you know you are aware, you will soon be defending your lunacy after you have your first Lucid dreams. It won't take long before you realize that your first Lucid dream was a success. I am dreaming!"

Think at Any Rate 2 Times Each Day

It is vital to have a clear head when you go to sleep, especially if you are trying to Lucid Dream. Contemplation is a way to maintain sanity. Mental well-being should be a goal for everyone. It opens doors to other life paths, such as how you can dream.

Think about it once per day, at any time that is convenient for you. Afterward, think about it again for 30 minutes before you go to bed. This contemplation technique should allow you to take a lot of time to reflect on your day, and then get it all in order before you embark on your Lucid dreaming ventures. Get supplements that help you to Lucid Dreaming

This is not a major step in your path to prosperity. However, dreams upgrading enhancements can improve your state of profound rest (REM) or rapid eye movement (REM). This is the place where you are most likely to dream. The more helpful you are, the more valuable your fantasies cycles.

You should make it a habit to start by taking a multivitamin each day. Also, be sure to include magnesium, choline, or fish oil. All of these nutrients will aid in sound cerebrum functioning. The tranquilizer melatonin, which is also very effective, is another option. If you are experiencing any side effects or have taken any medication, consult your primary doctor before you start any new enhancements.

Mellow can be a practice that you do, quietly or loudly, right before you go to bed. Recite the phrase "I will dream this evening and I will know it is dreaming" again and again until your float away. Your memory aid state should be compared with the one below. The more you can identify your practice with it the more impressive it will become.

You shouldn't be confused if your Lucid dreams don't come as quickly as you wish. Although there are good chances that you will be able to dream Lucidly if these rules are followed, there is no guarantee. Like many things in everyday life, you are more likely to be Lucid when you dream.

Understanding Your Fantasy & Its Signs

The use of dream signs as a method to achieve Lucid Dreaming is another option. Like state checks, the process involves working with dream signs in the morning and then expanding your training into the late hours of the night. It's a combination of daytime and nighttime practice. It is possible to work with dream signs by becoming more aware of strange or fanciful occasions in the day and using those occasions as triggers for leading state checks. The illusory idea of what you have experienced is a key impetus for activating clarity. LaBerge refers this to a "fantasy induced Lucid dream," which means that you are using fantasy's substance as a catalyst for clarity. We are often able to see the dream we are having when we say to ourselves: "Goodness, this is very peculiar... I should dream." The strangeness of it all enlightens. When you notice a fleeing bird or book falling from the shelf, grab your camera and take a moment to consider whether this is a fantasy. Every time something strange happens, ask yourself "Is that a fantasy?" Dreaming can cause us to experience many strange phenomena, such as sudden changes, discontinuities or unusual events. There are many dreamlike experiences that may occur, such as flying, seeing pink elephants and running over anything. These are acceptable if we accept them as we tend to do.

There are many types dream signs. The first is the "frail" dream sign. These are rare, yet not impossible, dream events that occur in dreams. Although it is quite strange to see a strange dog enter your fantasy home, it is also not impossible. These are "solid" dream signs that only occur in fantasy. It's similar to when a chair becomes a pontoon. Or you end up flying. Individual dream signs are most useful. These are routine situations, people, and items that you see in your dreams. You can use repetitive dreams in this area. You can keep track of the events, people, entities, and activities in your fantasy journal to become more familiar with them. To trigger clarity, use your acclimation when they occur in your fantasies. His essence can be used as a sign you are dreaming. "Dream topics" can also be associated with dreams signs. To get comfortable with your mundane dreams subjects, which are all the things, characters, items, or situations that occur every day, you need to be comfortable. This can be done by going through your fantasy diary and looking for repeat topics. For example, if you dream of being pursued or being late for a flight, this topic can be used to help you get to the place you're actually dreaming. "Remember that I've been pursued like this before... Hold on for a second. I've been pursuing like this before... I should have a dream."

For half a month, you can save a diary and start to see designs. Your fantasy sign may be close at hand. For example, you may have a dream sign that is repetitive and has been with your whole life. You may find that your dream signs change as you go through life, such as when you meet new people or become a chief. Find a highlighter, go through your fantasy journal, and start underlining any articles, places or people that appear more than once. Keep track all of these fantasy signs.

Knowing how to recognize dream signs will help you prepare your subliminal for when they are present. For instance, if you find that you often dream about your ex, this could be a trigger to make sure you are aware that it is you who is dreaming. Be clear before bed that you will remember when you see your ex that I am dreaming. The easiest way to know that you're dreaming is by knowing that your fantasies communicate with each other in a familiar language.

Lucid Dreaming is a system that can be used to start Lucid Dreaming. Lucidly imagined the greater part of the members during a record-breaking success rate in just seven day without outside mediation.

Lucid dreams are when the visionary can see what they are seeing and have some control over how it unfolds. Science confirms the existence of legends. Science has discovered that Lucid dreams do exist. There are a few ways to create the possibilities people will experience.

Chapter 9: Do's And Don'ts To Lucid Dreaming

As with all things, lucid visioning takes practice. It is easy for people to get excited about the idea of experiencing lucidity. They may also expect to have a lucid nightmare the first time they attempt it. These are the common mistakes novices make when trying to lucid-dream.

* A lack or commitment to learning and experiencing lucid dreamsing. Just as it is difficult to learn and master other skills, such as instruments or sports, so it is with lucid visioning. Frustration can be part of the learning curve. Some people won't experience their first lucid dream until several months after they begin trying. The key to success is patience. Consistency and practice are equally important. You'll eventually get what your looking for.

* Getting Too Excited – Another mistake that would-be lucid dreamsers make is getting too excited. Sometimes it is difficult for people to see the value of taking the time to be patient in a world where so much pressure is placed on us to get what we want right away. To simplify the process of lucid dreaming, there are a few tricks that can help. If we want to attempt to dream clearly, we have all of these tools in our arsenal and are ready to fire any shots that are presented to us. You can relax by trying out different techniques at once. This will help to calm down and keep your mind focused on what you are dreaming.

* Rude awakenings: This is the term that we use to refer to people who are unable or unwilling to sleep for a full nights. There are many reasons that you may get woken up or disturbed at night. This will also disrupt the REM cycle which can then cut

down on any lucid dreams you may be having. These rude awakenings can be avoided by closing your windows and using a blanket.

* Dream retention - If a person is unable to recall their dreams properly, both the quality and ability to lucidly dream can be affected. This is especially true when using the Wake Back to Bed method (WBTB), in which one wakes up in the middle or a sleeping cycle to go back to bed in a state where luciddreaming occurs. When one wakes up using the WBTB technique and cannot remember what they dreamed, then it is difficult to expect dreams to continue when they fall back asleep. A dream journal is recommended to help you have more lucid dreams, or make it easier to get your first lucid one. Keep it near your pillow, and write in your dream journal immediately after you wake up.

* Take it step by step - People who experience lucid dreams may get overexcited and expect to jump from Mount Everest. Slowly and steadily work your way up to bigger goals. If climbing is something you are interested in, don't expect Mount Everest to be your first lucid vision. Instead, climb a ladder. Lucid dreamers often have such high expectations that they don't realize how difficult it can be to grasp the concept.

* Lust — Many people are drawn to the idea of lucid visioning due to all the possible sexual adventures that they could have. If you are able to learn about Lucid Dreams, you will be able to conjure Christian Grey and his red-room of pain. Also, you will find many other models of sexually appealing men for your needs. But, this simulation requires advanced knowledge in the field of Lucid Dreams and is not something you can do the first

time you fall asleep. It's not something you should do immediately. It is common to get too excited by all the sensuality and feel numb.

* Lucid Dreaming - When one is just starting to learn how lucid dreaming works, particularly when one doesn't have the practice or knowledge of the techniques, we often fall asleep chanting "lucid lucid lucid dreams, lucid lucid lucid lucid lucid lucid lucid lucid lucid lucid lucis." So much so, instead of falling asleep to lucid dreams, we drift off to dreaming of lucid lucid lucid lucid lucid lucid lucid lucid lucid lucide lucid lucid lucid lucid lucid lucid lucid lucid lucid lucies

The belief that lucid dreaming can help us become more in touch with our inner selves, and thus have more control over our true selves, is supported by the knowledge they have about how we perceive emotions and what we see. It is essential to understand your dream self. This is your inner self that is not the same as you are in waking life. Knowing the difference between dreams is like knowing the difference between waking and dream states. This knowledge will help you to recognize the beginning and continuity of proper awareness.

Chapter 10: Meditate Your Way To Lucid Dreams

Meditation is more beneficial than lucid-dreaming. It is important for your overall health that you take a few minutes each day to fully appreciate your body, and give it quality time. This can be achieved through yoga, guided meditation and meditative breathe. Although these are just a few options for meditation, they are an excellent way to start your journey to lucid sleep. Let's face it, we all do a lot. There are many things you do in your day. Meditation is a great way to unwind and find some peace. Who wouldn't want that?

Meditation is an integral part of WILD, as we've already discussed. It goes hand-in-hand with MILD which is another form mentioned earlier in this book. Meditation can be used to improve your in-dream skills like visualization and focused states. These are the keys to lucid dreams that will last longer.

The science backs this up. These studies support the direct connection between meditation, lucid dreaming and meditation. Both of these require you to be more aware, reflect, and focused. Meditation can help improve your ability to recall dreams. This is critical for lucid Dreaming.

Let's look into what meditation is. Meditation has been practiced at least for five-thousands of years. Nearly all religions practice some form meditation. Meditation doesn't require that you be religious. Psychophysiology is the foundation of meditation. This branch of psychology examines how the mind can influence the body. To be able to meditate your way towards lucid visioning, you will need to master two skills that are completely opposite each other. FOCUS, a higher degree mental concentration, are these skills. The second skill you need is QUIESCENCE. This is when your mind is quiet and calm.

Meditating doesn't mean you have to cut back on your family's time or disrupt your social life. Here are two simple ways to meditate: breathe to calm the mind, and do guided meditation to focus your attention. Both can be very relaxing and a great way of getting out of the daily routine. Even if it's only for a few minutes.

Breathing is the first type of mediation. The first form of mediation is simply breathing. Meditating requires different breathing techniques, but it is simple.

Find a quiet place. This kind of meditation requires that your back is straight. You can choose to sit on the floor or in a seat. You should keep your straight back straight to avoid falling asleep while you meditate.

Keep your eyes closed and pay attention to your breaths. You won't be able to control your breathing at first. You can just observe the pattern. Is your breath rapid, shallow, deep? Be aware of how your body moves with air.

It's normal to feel agitated and confused when you first start to meditate. That's okay. It is why you meditate. It's normal to feel that your mind is busier than usual. It's a sign you are increasing self-awareness. You are starting to notice how many thoughts and ideas you have. Impressive, isn't it? You should avoid following those thoughts. It would distract from your focus. Pay attention to your breath and how it moves through your nose.

If you find your mind wandering at any time, return to your center and concentrate on your breathing. It may take you ten to 15 minutes to get to the quiet state you want. When you achieve this state, your thoughts, although still active and at the forefront of your minds, will be clear and lucid. For as long you feel comfortable, stay in this state. You can also leave the state for as short a time as you like. Do this form of meditation each day. You can practice it before going to bed at night or the first thing in your morning. These are the most convenient as life's busy schedules can make it hard to take time out and meditate. You may find that you can meditate more easily if you take some time off from the hustle and bustle of your day. This breathing technique is great for anxiety. Deep, slow breathing is a way to get rid of stress's adrenaline rush.

Guided meditation, the next form of meditation, is also known. This is where you'll focus your attention. Again, find a quiet spot to sit down. Make sure to keep your spine straight so you don't fall asleep. Guided meditation increases self-awareness. It will allow you to separate yourself from your physical body.

Guided meditation is a place where you can use imagination. Imagine you are walking through a beautiful meadow. The sun is shining and the flowers are in full bloom. It's peaceful and tranquil. Inhale slowly, letting the fresh air inhale into your lungs. Take a moment and fully appreciate your surroundings.

The purpose of this technique is to use the power of visualization to expand your awareness of your imaginary landscape. This process will help you let go of all your day-to-day worries and thoughts. The blissful silence will be all you hear. You may be able hear birds singing, thunder or raindrops falling on the ground. The more mental imagery you can create, the better you will be.

As you begin to sink deeper into your meditation, notice the grass beneath your feet. Slow down and take a deep breath. Your movements in this state should always be slow and deliberate. Here you are free to enjoy the beauty of the world around you and take your time. It is okay if it helps you move instead of stopping often. This is your choice. This is your practice. You can do whatever feels right and what will help you meditate the most. Sometimes the scenery might change. That's OK. You just need to be aware of the change as you go along. Be aware of how the scene changes. This is the key element to self-awareness that allows for lucid dreaming.

To enter the deep, trancelike state, guided can take up to fifteen to twenty minute. Once you get there, your body will be completely unconscious and you may feel as if you are floating on another plane of existence. It is a beautiful and liberating experience. You can live in this state for as many years as you like. There are no limits. There are no limits. You won't get a genuine, guided meditation otherwise. You should try to stay there for at least a few minutes while you are there. This is about you. Take the time to take a break.

After you have been in a guided meditative state of mind for a reasonable time, you can gently awaken yourself from that state. It is important not to wake yourself up from this state. Take deep inhalations and count backwards to ten. One slow, deep breathe for ten. Next, inhale nine times. You can then take another couple of minutes to come out from the meditative states. It will give you the time your body needs to adjust back to reality.

These two self-guided exercises will help increase your self-awareness. They help you focus your attention without distraction. It can be unique and you can change the scene from time to make things more exciting. You can create your own out-of-this world scenes. Relaxation is key. Meditation wouldn't work if the scene you are in involves inter-galactic battles. The goal is to stimulate vivid mental imagery, while maintaining calm relaxation.

Last note: Meditation is a topic that needs to be addressed. If concentration is difficult, you can try a variety of meditation aids. Pandora has a lot of free sounds. Even though the free version is great, be aware that commercial interruptions can occur, so you might not get the best results. You can also download any of the meditation apps to you smartphone. Some are free with no advertisements, others cost up two bucks. Muse is a brand new product. It is a meditation headset which can make meditation much easier. The brain-sensing headband gives real time feedback on the state of your brain. Although this is expensive, it only costs two-hundred five dollars.

Chapter 11: The Phases A Sleep Cycle

After our discussion, we learned that dreams are images and stories that our brains create when we're asleep. They come in many different forms. Some are short while others can last for hours. Others are more frightening than others. Some may be exciting and some disturbing. These events cause the victim's senses to be temporarily numb. The person experiencing them cannot see, hear, taste or smell anything in that instant. In reality, he must be unconscious. This is because he is being transported in deep sleep. This means that he has virtually no control over what happens in the dream.

Two Methods of Dream Analysis: One and Two

The subject of dreams has been studied extensively by man throughout the centuries. Because dreams have existed as long as humankind has existed, they are a part of everyday life. Because dreams are part of everyday life for everyone, you can't separate men and them. These two (individuals as well as dreams) are so close that people have sought to understand the act of dreaming through many different methods. Despite all our efforts, we only have a limited understanding of the phenomenon. There are two kinds of dream analysis.

The neuroscientific perspective is more concerned with the logistics aspect dreams. It includes their production and organization as well as their characteristics and structure. One of their most well-known findings is that almost all dreams take place in a certain stage of each person's sleep. That phase is the Rapid Eye

Movement (REM). However, psychoanalysis goes far beyond this. It focuses on dreams' meanings and attempts at relating them to the dreamer. Psychoanalysts think that their method works better for people, as it tries to improve lives using the messages and lessons that are gleaned from dreams. Psychoanalysis is the predominant philosophy of most dream therapy, religious, and psychological schools.

Dream Facts

It is known that people dream every day. For an average night of 8 hours sleep, they will experience 3 to 6 dreams. Each one lasts at most five minutes. While the longer ones can last as long as 20 or 30 minutes, they all have a minimum duration. Even though they are more common than others, most dreams people have are not remembered once they are awake. It is not uncommon for people to forget that they dream often. Many deny even that they dream.

If you pay more attention to dreams, it can help you discover more about your undiscovered self. Because dreams are a demonstration of the relationship between the conscious and unconscious minds, this could lead to you learning more. It can help one move toward wholeness as it exposes other unknowns about themselves. Long-term memory development can be aided by relating more to your dreams. Your memory retention can be improved by having a long-term habit of keeping track on small details. Your intelligence will improve when you are able to connect multiple facts between your unconscious, conscious, or subconscious states.

There is evidence that women are more concerned about their children and homes than they are about their family. This is due to the fact they are more at home, and therefore tend to run most of the domestic affairs. The men are different. Men are different. While they spend time with their family at home, their attention is often elsewhere: likely in their careers, businesses and projects. This means that men are more likely to dream in the direction of these other things. These tendencies show that a lot of what we think about in our dreams is related to how much time we spend thinking about it. If you watch many movies, there is a good chance that your dreams are affected by the same effects.

There are several stages of sleep that every person experiences. We'll be discussing these shortly. But, the Rapid Eye Movement stage (REM) is the most suitable for dreams to take place. Non-Rapid Eye Movement sleep phases are not as conducive to dreaming as the REM.

Even though some dreams might still appear in non-REM periods of sleep, their quality is not as good as that of the REM. There is a wide range in the quantity and quality of the dreams in REM and nonREM phases. That's why those who sleep longer at night experience more dreams than those who sleep less or have interrupted sleep.

It has been shown that 48% of people who appear in dreams are familiar with the individuals. 52% may be unknown individuals the dreamer might not have seen or contacted before. But, dreams can alter the appearance or form of people so that we don't recognize them. The world of dreams can be a puzzle. It is not surprising that man continues to try to solve it. There have been numerous instances in which dreamers are involved with their dreams, but with different bodies or faces. They might not recognize themselves, but their inner being (personality) will remain the same. This is also why they are key figures in the whole scenario.

People with blindness have more dreams then those who have sight. Their surroundings are often unrestful and accompanied by noise, noise, tension, and movement. Their ears are only open to receiving information from the surrounding environment. Because of this, they are more able to maintain calm and composure than those who see and hear. People who are more peaceful are more likely to remember and dream about the past. Blind people are kept out of most of the happenings in the outer world. They tend to move inwards the more and blend in. If they don't put in the effort to strengthen their vision, those who see will tend to be more dependent on their senses that what their subconscious and unconscious minds transmit. Therefore, their propensity to dream is reduced.

People are affected in many ways by hard and/or alcohol drugs, including their sleep. Alcohol and hard drugs have an impact on almost all aspects of a person's sleep. This includes their drowsiness prior to sleep, duration, and depths of sleep. It is common for any factor that affects sleep to have an effect on dreams. The dream's quality and contents might be less than usual. This effect is unknown. It is also not known what dream contents will result from the consumption of alcohol or other drug substances.

These are the most basic facts you need to know about dreams. We will be looking at how dreams relate to each phase of a person's sleeping habits.

The Phases of A Sleep Cycle

A complete sleep cycle is one that includes a full night of rest, not just a brief nap in the afternoon. A full cycle should have five cycles. They are what are they, and how do they differ from one another.

1. Phase 1

This stage is not the end of a person's normal sleep cycle. You can quickly wake up from this stage. However, some people may lose their ability to fall asleep again. This is the pre-sleep period. There is usually a slight release from the brain into the sleeping realm. As its activities stop, the eyes might be moving slowly and the muscles may slow down. This phase is about 5% to the total cycle of sleep. It is very difficult for dreams to come at this stage.

2. Phase 2

This stage is where the individual goes deeper into sleeping. His awareness of the world around him increases, and he is completely unaware of it unlike the first stage. This is when the eyes stop moving. The brain continues its activities but its electrical functions, known as brainwaves, slow down. There are only a few brief bursts of brain waves known as sleep spindles. This phase of sleep is responsible for between 45 and 55% of the total sleeping cycle.

3. Phase Three

The third period of sleep takes up about 4 to 6 % of the overall duration. Although it is shorter than the other two, it is also deeper and more enjoyable. The person has entered a more restful phase. As the brain slows down, the erratic brain waves fade. This aids to sleeper sedate and calms the mind. Despite these very slow brain waves, there are still faster waves, which appear at periodic intervals.

4.Phase Four

At this stage, sleep is very deep and resounding. It's not easy to wake from this stage. A person who is awakened at such a stage will never be alert or sharp, at least in the immediate future. It will take time for his sleepiness to fade and for him be awake again. The brain releases delta waves during this time. The minor body activities like eye movements, muscle activity and other activities that were characterized by stages one and 2 cease to exist. The stage 4 comprises approximately 12 to 15% the duration of the sleep period.

5.Phase Five - The Rapid Eye Movement Stage

This is the final and fifth stage of a sleeping cycle. It takes up between 20 and 25% of your total sleep time. This phase almost eliminates the calmness of the previous two. The sleeper will have more rapid, irregular breathing and shallower breathing. There could also be eye jerking, as well as limbs remaining motionless and moving in a fast manner. Everything appears to be alive and active. There is an increase in blood pressure, increased heart rate, and penile erection for male sleepers. The majority of dreams are experienced in this phase. If the sleeper awakens in this phase, he might feel more alert and strengthened to move about the day.

This chapter is about the realities of dreams. We may have gained a greater understanding of the world and its dreams at this point. This summit takes us to the next segment that focuses on techniques for analyzing dreams.

Chapter 12: Benefits And Lucid Dreaming

Now that we've talked about lucid waking, do you still wonder why? You probably have realized the many benefits and hundreds of reasons to continue lucid waking. You can learn more about lucid dreams and why it is so important for everyone, regardless of whether you are just starting out or have been doing it for years.

Improvements in Your Life

The first is that it enhances your life and career without adding extra work. It frees you up to do things you may not be able to or want to. You can do it while you sleep. Even if you have dreams, you can still get lucid. There are techniques that take very little effort to get lucid. You have no excuse not to do it. You would be able enjoy your dreams while also using them to advance your life.

How to Know Yourself Well

Lucid dreams can be a fascinating way to learn more about yourself, how your mind works, and even how you see the world. This is a big revelation for many people. It's possible to be in a place that you can never lose and your fears of failure will disappear.

While many people are able to imagine it, the mind is the best way to create reality. It is one thing to imagine something. But it is quite another to actually feel the things you are thinking. Everything feels real and real in a lucid vision. Remember that even your brain can believe everything is happening.

The possibilities are endless when we interact with our dreams.

Skill Acquisition

This benefit is one the most well-known uses of lucid visioning. This is used to develop real-life skills. An example of this is perfecting your form when you lift weights in the gym. It is possible to lift a weightlift in a dream but you don't use your muscles. You won't be able to build muscle. You're not burning extra calories, so you won't lose any real weight.

What you're really doing is firing off the exact same neurons when you attempt to perform that lift in real world.

With this knowledge, you can practice the techniques. A lot of research has been done with athletes who use lucid-dreaming to improve their real-world abilities.

Surprisingly, this skill is not new. It actually dates back to ancient times. People have been doing it for centuries, and have developed years of visualization skills and lucid visioning. Modern techniques have made this easier, but the only difference is in how they research it.

You can now experience lucid dreams instead of just thinking about it.

Better Sleep Habits

It can also help you look forward and build better sleep habits. Apart from the rare occasions when we feel tired or need to rest, most people don't really look forward much to sleeping. While we look forward to having more time to enjoy our lives and to being able to relax and have fun, a lot of people do not believe that sleep is important. You see, many people stay up too late to get to sleep. It almost feels like we don't want it to end. There is a good chance that many of us would agree to a deal where we could be awake all day without sleeping. This can lead you to develop bad sleep habits. Funny thing is, I have been guilty of this myself. Over the years, I had terrible sleep habits. Part of that was because I didn't want to go sleep. Learning to lucidly dream was the solution. It was because there was something that I could do while I was sleeping. I got to do the things I wanted to do while I was sleeping.

All of these things suddenly gave me reason to be excited about sleep. This resulted me in taking better care my sleep habits.

Mood Improvement

Lucid dreaming also has the added benefit of making you happier. When you wake up after having lucid visions, you may feel more relaxed. It feels great to wake up. These dreams are yours to share with others; you want them to be written down. You're excited for the next adventure. What are your plans for the next step? A lot of times, you have made some progress. You might have an idea for a dream control strategy, and you tried it. And all those steps, all those little changes, all those exciting experiences, those were all very important. You wake up feeling excited, happy and ready to face the day. It is an excellent moodlifter.

Eliminating negative emotions

Lucid dreams can help people overcome major negative emotions as well as boost positive ones. Fear is one the biggest negative emotions. Fears can be defeated by Lucid Dreaming. It is possible to confront fear in your lucid nightmare in a safe and secure environment that won't harm you. The lucid vision creates a safe space that removes risk. In the dream you will realize that you can make anything scary go away at any time. You can also wake up whenever you want. Whatever fear you have, you can overcome it in the dream by taking small steps until you conquer the fear. It is possible to do things that you cannot do in real life.

Let's just say that you are afraid to touch spiders. In real life, there are unlikely to be a million spiders for you to take a shower with. Exposed yourself in dangerous ways is not an option. However, dream control allows you to make the bath look like it's full of spiders. You can also use your subconscious mind to create suggestions and make drastic changes in your dreams, because you're engaging with it so much.

The best part is that you don't have only to face fears in your dreams. You can also implant suggestions to help make you more confident and to help you face your fears in the real world. This does not only work for fears. These elusive dreams are able to help you overcome other negative emotions.

Lucid dreams can be used to reprogramme your subconscious and have therapeutic benefits. Lucid dreams can be used to your advantage as a tool.

Memory Improvement

The next is that it can help improve memory. Things are easier to recall if there is an emotional effect. It's not possible to form strong memories by simply reading a paragraph in the book. You will always remember the lesson you learned from that paragraph of a book if it is an emotional experience.

This allows you to take what you've studied and transform it into real life experiences in your dreams.

They stimulate all your senses, and also engage your emotions. However that is not all you can do for lucid dreams. If you're having lucid dreams, you may be keeping a dream diary. It's a great way of improving your memory. Normally, we have very little access when we're asleep to that part of our brain. Many people remember only a few dreams each night.

If you begin a dream journal, you will have better access to your subconscious memory. It is the place where deeper memories are stored. You should see an improvement in your memory.

Lucid dreaming can help you improve your memory.

Lucid Dreaming is an effective way to access your deepest memories. It is created by the subconscious and the dream world around you. It is possible to draw it incorrectly from memory. However, this memory can be found in your subconscious, and you can create an exact representation with very few errors. It's because your subconscious knows it.

Your subconscious has an almost photographic memory of everything.

The reason is that conscious access to most of the information in our brain is limited. 99 percent times, we have only access to the relevant information our brain believes is important for us to know.

With some clever tricks and dreams control, it is possible to access many of your memories and retrieve any information you forgot.

Total Freedom and Fun

All the experiences you desire are possible. Through practice, you can transform your subconscious into an imaginative mental playground. Dream control allows you to meet anyone, travel through the stars, and live out your wildest fantasies.

No limits! No consequences! No holding back!

E

You will be amazed by the amazing things your brain can create: detailed imagery, smells and sounds, as well as tastes. It is possible to experience intense physical sensations.

Nightmares: How to Get Rid of Them

The treatment of nightmares is the next benefit to lucid dreamsing. Many people have problems with nightmares and fear. Sometimes it steals their sleep. Because the dreamer has control over the dream and the sleep, Lucid Dreams can be used to overcome such fears.

Therefore, the dreamer no longer becomes a helpless victim. Lucid dreaming is a way to end nightmares. Let me explain.

The ability to discern between real life and dreams is what a lucid dreamer achieves. They become conscious and can tell when they are dreaming from reality. These people can recognize when they have nightmares and may just choose to look at the movie as a way to see how they feel. Other ways are that they can completely control the dream. They can have total control of the vehicle and take it to wherever they please.

Creative Leaps

Strange things seem normal in a lucid nightmare. You can defy physical laws or create entirely new life forms. The number of fish that each candidate can catch with their naked hands from a standard swimming pool can determine whether you can alter the course of time or who becomes the next president. Interesting, right? Anything can happen.

It's possible, as long you can imagine it.

This will amaze you at the creative and imaginative ways your brain can function in lucid sleep.

It is possible to dream lucidly, but logic barriers have been removed. This makes it easier to think outside of the box and create amazing stories. New story ideas, business solutions, insights, and new ways of tackling problems are possible. It's no surprise that research has shown that people who lucidly conceive of new ideas, business solutions, insights for work and entirely new perspectives on solving problems is much more common than people who don't.

Chapter 13: What Is Required For A Dream Life?

As with any skill, dreaming clearly takes effort and patience. It is common knowledge that it would take ten thousand hours to master a skill depending on how gifted you are. Even if mastery is your ultimate goal and proficiency is your primary goal, it's impossible to learn the skills to mastery without practicing them. Without practice, no matter what you learn about lucid visioning, the performance will end up being a disaster.

This guide will cover all the necessary skills to enable you to have lucid dreams. The following is a brief outline of the process. The outline of the process, compiled from the experiences of successful Lucid Dreamers, is not to be skipped. You must integrate these basic skills into your daily life before induction techniques can be practiced.

1. It is important to remember your dreams. You will not be able, before you start to train to reach lucidity. It is possible for the dream experience to fade into the distractions of daily life if it is not possible to recall.

2. Analyse your dream patterns: Take a close look at your dreams and how you've recorded them. This will help you to find trends within your dreams. It is important to identify the "dream signs" as they will help you see what you are dreaming.

3. Training yourself to validate reality: There are many reality checks that you can use to confirm if you're in a dream. These checks must be incorporated into your daily life to ensure that they are successful.

Each of the skills required to induct lucid dreams will be thoroughly examined before we move on to examine other induction techniques. Understanding how our sleep cycles work will improve your chances of having memorable, and hopefully, lucid dreams.

A longer sleep time per night will lead to a longer REM period. This will allow for more deep (and longer-lasting) dreams. If you are trying to have a lucid dreams, it is important that you do not sleep more than nine hours. Longer REM cycles can be achieved by sleeping longer. These happen in ninety-minute intervals.

A great way to help yourself pay more attention to your dreams is interrupting your REM, as this is the only way to recall them. Many recommend setting your alarm in intervals between ninety and six minutes, for example, after you go to sleep, at four and a 1/2, six, or seven-and-a half hours. You must master each skill before you can attempt to induce lucidity.

Remember your dream

It is essential to be able to remember your dreams when you learn lucid-dreaming. A frustrating feeling is the one where you wake up from what seems like an incredible dream, but can't remember anything. Aside from the frustration of forgetting a dreams can cause other issues. Recovering from sleep in an effort to continue a dream can result in waking up at the alarm and then falling asleep. Important note: "Remembering your dreams can be the first step to having lucid dream experiences." It doesn't matter if you remember your dreams or not, but lucid dreams won't stick in your mind if it isn't.

It is possible that you are asking yourself how to start remembering what your dreams are. A dream journal is the most effective and recommended way to record your dreams. This works exactly as it sounds. It is important to write down your dream as soon as possible. This sounds very daunting.

But don't lose heart. It is important to take the time to reflect on the dream you have just had before you write it down. It is important not to move too much in this step. Instead, try to remain still. Review the details of the dream in your head. Take your eyes off of the screen and look at the imagery. Use the imagery that you have recalled to associate with any other dreams. The "essential criterion of lucid dreams" is the dream journal.

Even if you only have fragments of your dreams to recall, keep a diary near your bed.

While you may not recall many details the first time you start, you will get better at it as you practice. Take a look at each sense. Can you recall anything you felt, heard, saw, touched or tasted during the dream? Keep track of everything that you can. It will teach your brain that the senses matter and are worth remembering.

You can keep a dream diary for when you attempt to lucidly dream later. Even though you may feel tired, you should get up from your bed and keep your excitement about what you want to have lucid dreams about.

Remember to first review your dreams when you wake up. Then, write down the dream. Give each dream a "catchy subtitle" to help you remember it later. In addition to the date and the time it occurred, details should be given about the experiences and images that you remember.

It can be tempting just to note down your dreams on scraps. You will be able to remember all your dreams better by simply noting their importance, as the above exercise suggests. You should keep all your dreams together in a book or notebook that can be used only for them. At first, it might be difficult to keep track of enough information to fill the back of a receipt. However, if you work hard, you will be able to write pages about your dream every night. Or expand on the ones you already have. Finally, having all your dreams in one spot gives you an organized way to perfect the next step.

Identify your dream signs

As your ability to recall your dreams improves, you will notice patterns in your dreams. You will find it useful, although not necessary, to revisit your dream journal. Seek out recurring elements. For example, a friend of mine shared that water is a common element in her dreams. A lot of dreamers have a dark cinematographic feeling. It's as if everything is happening under a very dark shadow. These indicators can appear in a variety of ways. Some are permanent, others are intermittent. Although dreams can have a shadowy feeling, there is likely to be a theme of movement or transport, often at very high speeds, like when you are on a high speed train.

It is important to pay attention to emotions in dreams. These may also indicate a dream condition. This could indicate that you are dreaming.

Post continues his instructions regarding dream journaling. Here he shares some information about what he believes dream sign to be. If you look at your description of the dream, you will be able to identify context clues that might indicate that you were dreaming. Post dreams that the dreamer is back at school in French.

The setting of the dream, his high-school, should be an indicator that he was actually dreaming. Recording the patterns or themes within these dream signs will increase your likelihood of being able to recognize them while you are asleep, which can help induce a lucid state. You are training your mind to recognize these signs during your daily life.

The interesting thing about this is that it reminds us that dream signs are not something we seek out during sleep. This will allow us to be open to even the most unlikely ideas. Dreams can allow us to accept any situation without questioning. It's like watching ourselves in a movie that doesn't limit us.

It takes training to see and fully comprehend the dark corners of our dreams. We need to convince our minds that if you see something strange, then it is likely that we are dreaming.

If you first analyze them, the only way to subconsciously recognize dreams signs is to do so. You should also make it part your everyday routine to be on the lookout. If you start looking in the waking realm for patterns that you have observed in your dreams, your brain will automatically become more open to finding them. In this way, you can induce lucidity by looking around for inconsistencies that will alert you and trigger the state. Once you are trained to be aware and alert for dream signs, you can begin creating reality checks.

Reality checks

A reality check allows you to find out if your dream state is real or false. The reality check refers to an action or series actions that you take. It has a defined and known reaction when you are awake.

As dreams are often guided by their own internal logic, which may or might not be consistent with the context of the actual dream, it is possible to use such an action to test the world around you. While a reality check is a valid way to test your world in the real world, it may have weird or inconsistent results in a dream.

We will explore several tried and true reality checks. The second is to verify that you are dreaming.

Reality checks allow you to see how real the world is. However, reality checks only work when they are rooted within waking life phenomena. Some methods evaluate your body and abilities. Others can help you evaluate the world around. Post briefly discusses reality checks. Post specifically mentions the watch he wears constantly to look for irregular readings. If you've had a dream sign or a reality check, it can be used as another way to test your lucidity. Reality checks are often done using clocks.

Dream signs don't necessarily have to be exceptional, like flying, as long as they aren't connected with your normal, daily experiences. For example, the hands often appear blurry, or they have too many fingers or joints. Sometimes it's helpful to push one side of the other. In a dream, one side will pass through the other. This is not possible in the real world.

Because your body regulates its breathing regardless of your actions in the dream, your ability to breathe will not be affected by what actions you take. If you dream of being underwater or underground, your breathing will continue. You aren't preventing your body from regulating air intake.

Many people complain about inconsistency with technology. Post's example is that Post's watch will show a time and when Post looks away, it shows a different hour. Light switches are often described not as functional, or in the same way they work in the waking world. The light switch for your living area might turn on the light in your kitchen or illuminate a wall.

A final note: Text is often not as accurate as it should be. Read a page from a book you find. If you are looking at a book, look away. When you look back, make sure that the words on the page have not changed. In some cases, text can be hard to read due to strange characters.

It is important to perform reality checks every day of your waking life. You can make them a part of the dream experience by training yourself subconsciously to do them. Once you've identified your signs, it is possible to start reality checks whenever you see them. By recording our dreams and analysing them for patterns, we can discover how these three skills work together to create a lucid Dream.

It is best to be able to recognize that reality checks are simply reactions to stimuli, and not a deliberate, intelligent response. Sometimes, your dream signs may not be able to relate to the waking world. You should choose something that you see a lot in your waking life if you don't have the chance to encounter your dream sign often enough. Your reality check could be performed whenever you go into a structure or enter through a doorframe.

Final tip: You should do a reality checking every time that you wake up. It is not uncommon for lucid dreamers, who often believe they have awakened, but actually continue their lucid state to the point that they start their daily lives without ever getting out from bed.

As you practice, these checks will be automatic and you won't even think about why you do them. You may find yourself doing these checks while in a dream. Once reality checks become automatic, these subconscious reactions will be automatic. You will start to notice that sometimes you are conscious and aware that your dreams are real. You might suddenly wake-up.

These steps are effective in creating a dream. If you have been practising the initial steps, you may be familiar with what a lucid dream is and what you want to accomplish at night. You don't have to worry if you're not familiar with the first steps. The techniques below will help you achieve lucid dreaming.

Chapter 14: What Your Dreams Are Telling You, Interpreting Common Symbols. Dreams With Colors & Numbers.

Sometimes symbols and objects can make dreams very confusing. It is important for you to remember that dreams and meanings can be as individual as the people who dream them.

Some people interpret dreams only for fun. Other people take the meaning of dreams seriously and make them a part their lives. No matter what reason you have for dream interpretations, these common symbols can help you understand them.

Angels

An angel in your dreams can be a symbol of purity. It can also symbolize a desire for spiritual goodness or enlightenment. A lot of people who dream about angels as teachers or guides in their dreams take the advice of angels very seriously.

Animals

Animals are symbolic of intuitive emotions, desires, and actions. Sometimes our intuitions are suppressed because we have to follow a code for civilization in a society.

Each animal's dream meaning is different. Dreaming about cats is a way to suppress your feminine intuition. Dreaming about a lion symbolises repressing anger and/or repressing your desire to rule. It is crucial to pay attention to the specific traits of the animal in order to interpret your dreams about it.

Blood

The symbol of vitality and strength is to dream about blood. Dreams about blood depend on the context. As an example, blood in violet represents loss of control and disturbance in life. While a dream that involves bloody hands can be interpreted as guilt.

Illness

The dreaming of illness could be interpreted as your body telling you something is wrong. Your subconscious mind can sense things that your conscious mind may not.

Keys

The symbolism of dreaming about keys is keeping secrets, and it can also be used to symbolize fear of revealing a particular matter.

Locks

Dreaming of locks can signify that the dreamer isn't able to achieve his or her goals in life.

Mountain

A mountain climb can be symbolic of reaching new heights, setting goals and striving for success. If you dream of gazing at a mountain, it could be a sign that you are making a big decision in your personal life. Dreams of scaling a mountain represent the victory over unsurmountable odds.

Fog

The dream of fog represents a state where you feel lost and confused. But it can also be used to describe a desire for exploration of new parts of your personality or life.

Road

When you dream about the road, it symbolizes the direction of your life or your goal. A straight road indicates that everything will go well, while a bumpy path is indicative of problems in a certain area of your life.

Garden

It is symbolic of spiritual growth to dream about lush gardens. Dreaming of a dead garden, or a weed-infested garden is indicative that a dreamer seeks spiritual sustenance.

Being Chased

As well as a literal meaning, dreams of being chased might have a symbolic or literal meaning. The literal meaning is that a dreamer fears being a criminal victim. This fear is often more prevalent among women than for men.

It can cause fear, stress or pressure. You may feel like an attacker is chasing you in dreams. It is possible to resolve recurring dreams of being pursued by examining and confronting such issues in your actual life.

Death

The dream of dying is often interpreted as the possibility that you or someone close to your will die. It is rare that this is the case. However, dreams of death or dying are a sign that you may be experiencing anxiety & stress in real life.

Fire

Fire symbolizes passion, sexuality, and transformation according Carl Jung, a well known psychologist.

Falling

A dream about falling is a symbol of insecurity, instability, loss of control, helplessness, and lack of control in real life.

Failure

The dreaming of failure can take the form of failing tasks or failing tests. It can also be any task you attempt but fail to accomplish. Such dreams can signify being anxious, worried, stressed and anxious in your real world.

Flying

The most common dream of flying is one that is exciting and fun. It represents striving for perfection, but can also signify a strong sense control and a lack of power. Dreams of flying where you are able to control your speed and where you fly represent a strong sense control. However, if you dream that you have trouble flying and then fall to the floor, this is a sign that you lack control and feel powerless.

Rain

Rain is an element that symbolizes purity and renewal. However, meanings of rain can change depending on what context the dream is in. If you dream of seeing rain fall, it can be a sign of luck, fortune, or blessing. But if you dream of dark clouds and heavy rain, it could also indicate isolation, depression, or feelings of loneliness.

Running

Dreaming in a dream means that you are able to escape difficult situations in your real life.

Window

Perceiving through a window in a dream symbolizes the dreamer's perspective. The views you see and the emotions that accompany them will determine your viewpoint.

Abandonment

Dreams of abandonment, which are common in dreams, represent a dreamer's fear of being left alone in real life situations.

Desert or Island

Imagine yourself lost on an island or desert and you will feel lonely, confused, stuck and unsure of what to do.

Houses

The dream of living in the same house as your parents symbolizes a dreamer's desire to travel back in time. This can happen after marriage, graduation, or when you move to a new area.

Dreaming about threatening houses or unfamiliar homes is an indication of unwillingness or fear of change.

People

You see people in your dreams as manifestations or emotions of yourself. In most cases, the dream is about you and not the person you see in the particular dream. As a physical symbol of your thoughts, and desires, the people you see in a dream can be interpreted as such.

These people can be imagined by your thoughts. A movie star is an example of what you might dream about.

Interpreting dreams about people involves understanding their personality, traits, backgrounds, and applying them to you in the most direct way.

Job

Dreaming of being at the office often signifies that you are overwhelmed, stressed and overworked about your career. Also, such dreams are considered a sign to be more productive in work.

Arms

A dream about arms can signify your subconscious desire to live the life you want. To dream about your hands being tied symbolizes that you feel trapped and restricted in your own life.

Hands

Depending on the context of your dream, a dream about hands could have both positive and/or negative meanings. For example, if you dream of clasped hands it means unity and agreement. However, if you see your hands washing then it means that you have unresolved matters that you must resolve in your real life.

Immobility

To dream of feeling immobilized or paralyzed is to feel trapped in a situation. It can be a smothering partner, a stressful job, or anything in between.

Teeth

A dream about losing teeth could be about feeling embarrassed, ineffective, or ashamed. The first theory is that teeth enhance the physical beauty of people and can be lost to represent fear of becoming old or concern about your appearance. The second theory considers teeth as strong. They can be damaged or broken so loss of teeth can indicate weakness and inferiority.

Essen

Dreams of eating can symbolize your desire for intellectual & spiritual nourishment over physical nourishment. It can also signify that you want to be cared about.

Cars

Dreams of driving a vehicle symbolize your desire for freedom.

It is possible to have dreams about car crashes. As a passenger you can dream of losing control.

Ocean

Dreams that involve large water bodies or the ocean represent a dreamer's emotional state. Dreams of low waves or calm symbolize an emotional life. While dreams of high waves and chaos are indicative of emotional turmoil,

Being Naked

Clothes provide a concealment method. Being naked during a dream means that you are hiding something or that others are seeing right through you.

Colors and dreams

You can interpret your dream by using color. Below are common colors and what they might mean in a Dream.

Pink

Pink color symbolizes affection, kindness or love. It can also be used to indicate being in or healing with love.

Red

Red is a sign of passion and anger.

Black

Black symbolizes death, aging, and is considered to be a sign that it is dark.

Grey

Greys, which represent fear and confusion, are an intermediate color between black or white.

White

White is a color associated with purity. In a vision it can symbolize hope, knowledge, and confidence.

Green

Green represents harmony, reconciliation balance and renewal. These can be both physical and spiritual.

Blue

Blue symbolizes spirituality. A dark blue color that is a mix of blue and black is representative of fear, while a light blue color represents hope and belief.

Gold

The dream color gold is a sign of richness and enhancement, which could be in your surroundings or in your status.

Dreams about Numbers

Here are some numbers you might see in your dreams.

Zero 0

Zero is used as a symbol to denote emptiness. It could signify that your efforts in life are not working, or that you feel your life is headed nowhere.

One

One an odd number represents unity, togetherness, completeness.

Two

As an even number, it represents balance and equality.

Three

Three stands for vitality and energy. Three is a representation for trilogy & completion. This includes mind, body and soul. If you see Number 3 in a dream, it could be a sign that the third time is likely to prove lucky.

Four 4

Four stands for earthliness. This is the four elements of nature, fire and wind, as well hard labor. A dream that shows four represents hard work, stability, and the ability to achieve your goals.

Five 5

Five symbolizes the 5 senses (hear/touch/smell, taste/smell, sound/sound and taste). It is also a symbol of activity, adventure, and spontaneity. It could also signify new beginnings, growth or change in a dream.

Six 6

Six stands for domestic bliss, cooperation, and harmony. Dreaming 6 is a sign of domestic harmony and love for the future.

Seven 7

Seven stands for healing ability. If you see it in a vision, you know you are on the right road. Repeated 7's in dreams mean you are on the right track and will overcome all obstacles.

Eight 8

Eight stands for success and wealth. This number is associated to trusting your intuition. To see number eight in dreams means to trust your instincts, take action and believe in yourself.

Nine 9

Nine stands for reformation and rebirth. If you see this number in your dream, it means that you are reaching your full potential.

Ten 10

Ten means completeness and totality. A repeated number 10, can indicate perfection of a task, or situation in your life.

Chapter 15: Scheduling For Lucid Dream

Many lucid dreamers claim that their dreams happen in the early hours of the morning, after sunrise. The reason for this is because the second half is longer in REM than the first. A laboratory analysis of the time periods in which lucid thoughts occurred showed that the relative probability of lucid experiences increased with each successive REM interval. Let's suppose that you typically sleep for eight hours. During the night there are six REM cycles. Half of these occur during the last quarter. According to research, you have twice the chance of having lucid dream experiences in the last 2 hours of sleep than in your first 6 hours. This means that your chances of lucid vision will drop by half if you decrease your usual sleep time for two hours. If you have only six hours of sleep per night, you can increase your sleep by two hours to double your chance at lucid dreaming.

It's clear that you can encourage lucid-dreaming by increasing the amount of sleep. If you are very interested in lucid-dreaming and have more time, then schedule at least one morning each week. Even though most people want to sleep at night, it is not possible to find the time. There is an easy trick that will increase the frequency and duration of lucid sleep if you don't want to spend as much time at night. It doesn't require you to spend more sleep than usual. Reschedule how you sleep. Try to wake up at 4am if your usual sleep time is between midnight and 6:00 a.m. Keep awake for two hours, and you can do all that you need. Rest between 6:00 to 8:00 AM. Your REM will go to sleep for two hours longer than usual (6:00 - 8:00) and your chances of awakening with vivid dreams will increase.

Some lucid dreamers may arrange their sleep in a way that makes them more lucid. Worsley explained that Worsley wakes up at 1:30 am in the morning to start dreaming. He usually sleeps between 2:45 and 7:45. He then wakes up to have breakfast, tea, or read newspapers and mail. He usually stays awake for around two to three more hours. He would then write down details about the experiment or activity he wants to carry out in a dream. He usually falls asleep between 9:00 and 9:30. He then falls asleep for several hours. A great way to encourage lucid dreaming is to distribute sleep. This is something you should definitely try. You'll get a lot of return for your effort. This is a great way to help you get started.

Set up your Lucid Hour

1. Alarm

Before you go to bed, set the alarm so that you wake up 2 to 3 hours earlier than normal. After that, you will fall asleep at your regular time.

2. Wake up early in the morning

If the alarm begins to ring, get up immediately. You will be awake for approximately two to three more hours. Continue working until approximately half an hour before retiring to bed.

3. The realization of lucid dream is the goal

Before you fall asleep, spend half an hour contemplating what you wish to accomplish in your lucid dreams. These could include where you want go, what you want do, and who you want you to see. You can also use this time for dream incubation on specific topics. You can practice any application you are working on in this guide.

4. Return to bed to learn induction skills

After you've been awakened for at least two to three hour, go back to bed and ensure that your sleep area is peaceful and quiet for the following few hours. You can go to bed and test the sensing technique that you like best.

5. You should get at least two hours sleep

If you'd like, you can set the alarm or have someone wake it up for you. But, make sure to allow yourself two hours. You might have one or two more rapid eye movements.

Lucid dreaming can be done in the morning. We need at least an hour to enter REM sleep. However, most of us only reach REM after waking up. Sometimes we can wakeup from a dream, and then reenter it after a brief period. These facts make it possible to dream lucidly.

Deep Relaxation: Learn how to do it

Before you are able to practice techniques that induce Lucid Dreaming, you must be able to focus and relax. You also need to maintain a calm mind and relaxed body. Below are two ways to do it. They're important because they help to eliminate your day's worries so that you can be lucid. Lucid dreams require concentration. This is difficult for nervous and distracted bodies. These basic techniques should be learned before moving on.

Progressive Relaxation

1. Lying on a solid area

If you can't lie down, find a chair that is comfortable. Close your eyes.

2. Your attention should be on breathing.

Be aware of your breathing and try to deepen it. Move your diaphragm slightly down when you inhale. Push your abdomen forward and draw air into your lungs. Allow yourself to exhale and relax.

3. Gradually tighten, relax and tone each muscle group

Relax all muscle groups at once. Start with the dominant side. Start by bending your wrist backwards as if you were placing your back on your forearm. Tend for five to ten secs. Pay attention. Relax and relieve stress. Pay attention to the differences. Take a deep breath and let go of stress. For 20-30 seconds, pause while you take a deep breath. Then exhale slowly and replace your hand. Repeat the process for your forearm (upper arm), forehead, forehead and neck. Next, take a deep breath. Pause between each major muscle groups, take a deep breathe, and let go of more tension.

1. Let go

Continue to work all muscle groups. You can still relax and perform tension-relaxing sequences no matter where you are nervous. Your body will feel like it is flowing with tension. When you feel nervous or relaxed, remember that relaxation is stronger than ever before. The order of the points must be remembered. It is easy to remember the order of the points because they are fixed in a straightforward way. They start at the forehead, work their way down on the right side, cross to your left hand, lower body, left and right legs and finally reach the forehead.

2. Focus

Start with the forehead. Keep your eyes on the eyebrows, and then think about it. Keep your eyes on the eyebrows and think about where it is. Now think about where your location is. Before moving onto the next step you should feel heavy and warm in that place.

3. Each point is moved in turn

Keep your eyes on the important details. Begin slowly and visualize yourself at the point. Warm and heavy should be your first thought before you proceed. Don't let your mind linger. At first it might be difficult. If this happens, don't let your mind wander. If you are unsure of your position, return to the point you began or ended at and go on. Practice until you master each aspect of the subject.

4. Your practice should be extended to cover all points

If you're able to complete 31 points in a particular order, repeat steps 1-2 for each of the 61 points. To ensure you are able to reach all points, make it a habit and continue to do so until you lose focus. You can use this activity to induce lucid dreaming.

Chapter 16: Stepping Into The Dream World

Now that you've learned a lot about dreaming, it is time to move into the dream realm.

Because everyone dreams, and most people dream on a regular basis. It's not necessary to describe it. Even though you feel you are in the dream at times, most people don't realize that they're there. Your dream might look like a movie. You may be watching yourself in motion as though you are outside of your own body. This could be your personal perspective. It may seem like you are viewing it as a film.

You might find that this is different from one dream to another. However, we can remember the most intense dreams and the ones we recall most clearly when we are in the middle of it all.

First person view.

The first step is to recognize your dream state. Dreams are something we all recognize, but it is often not what we expect.

But it can be almost as real as everything else in your life. The colors, the sounds... everything is so vividly and clearly visible. You may even feel thoughts and fear.

However, now is the time to acknowledge that dream state.

Recognize the Dream State

We talked in chapter 3 about reality and dreamland. You were able to see the difference. You also learned the importance of asking yourself the question "Am I Dreaming?" consistently to create a habit.

Once you have made it a habit, it is likely that you will ask the same question during your dreams. Now you can take the information from your journaling exercise and use it to help you understand how all of this fits together. Analyze the senses: sight, sound and smell. Find out if you're dreaming.

You may feel a dream state is real for a short time. Although you can certainly wake up from a dream if it's true and you don't want the dream to continue, that doesn't mean you have control over the dream.

Lucid Dreaming is all about controlling the dream. It's the action you take that changes the dream's course.

Lucid dreaming can allow you to actually explore and take responsibility. You can meet up with people and memories you've forgotten. It is possible to unlock doors that have been shut down long ago.

However, the only way to do that is to be able identify your dream state.

Once you can see that you are dreaming, you will be able manage it.

It's all about practice.

Sometimes you might awaken from a dream when you start to see the reality of your dreams. Your brain could be trying to get you out of the dream by programming it to terminate it. Chapter 2 describes how your brain protects you from certain information stored in the subconscious parts of your mind. This information can be accessed during a dream state.

Keys for Lucidity When Dreaming

This revelation will allow you to realize that you are really dreaming. You can also have cogent thoughts that you manage. To benefit from this, you need to be lucid.

Lucid can be described as being 'expressed clearly and easily understood'.

Because dreams can be complex and confusing, as well as abstract, most people know this. It is a major turn on the notion of lucidity. However, once you are aware that you are dreaming, and you continue dreaming, you start tapping into higher levels of your subconscious and conscious minds.

If you have ever seen the movie "What Dreams May Come," with Robin Williams, Cuba Gooding Jr., then you will notice many of the scenes that are dreamlike. They represent the director's or, in the storytelling context, the character's idea of heaven. There are vivid colors... too bright, clear, and too many. It looks real. It feels real. It's not normal.

These scenes enable the characters to move. They can have conversations and talk, and even control what's being asked and said. They can also walk down hills or up. They can walk up and down hills.

If you are dreaming passively, you don't have any control. If you're lucidly imagining things, you'll feel more like a film director, controlling what you do, where you go and with whom.

Slow is the key to lucidity and a clear dream.

It's like learning algebra on a bike or a foreign language. It will take time to master it.

www.ingramcontent.com/pod-product-compliance
Lightning Source LLC
Chambersburg PA
CBHW050405120526
44590CB00015B/1840